KIDS SAY THE CUTEST THINGS

WHEN THEY'RE DRUNK

KIDS SAY THE CUTEST THINGS WHEN THEY'RE DRUNK

BY DAN McQUINN

A BOOK OF POINTLESS SATIRE AND VULGAR HUMOR

MOST OF IT FUNNY

This is a work of fiction. Names, characters, places and incidents are the products of the author's imagination or are used fictitiously. In fact, the author himself is a fictional person created from the mind of yet another fictional character. Any resemblance to actual events, locales or persons, living or dead, is entirely coincidental and pretty funny.

Kids Say the Cutest Things When They're Drunk
(A Book of Pointless Satire and Vulgar Humor, Most of It Funny)
By Dan McQuinn
Fauldhouse Publishing
Naperville, IL

All rights reserved. No part of this book may be reproduced or transmitted in any form or by any means, electronic or mechanical, including photocopying, recording or by any information storage and retrieval system, without written permission from the author, except for the inclusion of brief quotations in a review.

Unattributed quotations are by Dan McQuinn.

Copyright © 2011 by Dan McQuinn.

Edition ISBNs
Softcover 978-0-9832553-0-7
EPUB 978-0-9832553-1-4
First Edition 2011.

Printed in the United States of America.

Publisher's Cataloging-in-Publication Data
McQuinn, Dan.
  Kids say the cutest things when they're drunk : a book of pointless satire and vulgar humor, most of it funny / by Dan McQuinn.
  ISBN: 978-0-9832553-0-7
  1. American wit and humor. 2. Satire, American. I. Title.
PN6162 .M36 2011
817—dc22
2011920145

Book design by Christopher Fisher
Cover design by Dennis Marcellino

For Barb, Rose, and Jack

Contents

Preface	xi
Family	1
Guide to Parenting	3
How My Parents Met (As I Imagine)	16
Letter from Make-a-Wish	18
When Make-a-Wish Goes Bad	21
Divorce	22
Education	25
First Job	27
Seven Habits of Highly Effective Third-Grade Boys	29
Morning Visitor	30
Romeo and Juliet Essay Questions	32
A Very Brief History of Time	35
Take Our Daughters to Work Day	38
Highly Recommended	45

Biology	49
When I First Learned Where Babies Come From	51
A Conversation between the Two Cutest Girls on the High School Bus (As I Imagine)	52
Gone Fishing	55
First-Date Crib Notes	58
When I First Realized I Needed to Find a New College Roommate	60
Soul Mates	62
Christmas	65
Here Comes Santa Claus	67
Greetings from the McQuinns	69
Yankee Swap	72
Frugal Christmas Ideas	76
Enterprise	79
First Class (As I Imagine)	81
An Open Letter to the Employees of Chromatic Enterprises	84
Our Privacy Policy	88
Attitudes	93
Found in My Pocket	102
Circular Jerk	105
Order	111
Encyclopedia Brown Today: Solutions from the NYPD Case File	113
Henchman Wanted	116

Great Moments in the American Revolution (If I Were There)	120
Instructions for Voting	124
Vote for Bob	128
Celebrity	**131**
My Biopics, Reviewed	133
Couldn't Have Done It Without You	138
Now Playing	142
From the Notebook of Matt Damon	147
Why I Am the Funniest Person Alive	151
Miss You	154
Will Smith Haters Newsletter	158
God	**163**
Cain's New Girlfriend	165
Send in the Frogs	167
Inscriptions from Jesus' High School Yearbook	169
Gospel Writer's Group Feedback	173
What God Said to Me the Last Time I Prayed	176
The Good, the Bad and the Middling	177
Death	**179**
The First Telephone Conversation with my Mother after Nuclear Armageddon	181
When Death Gets Personal	184
How I Imagine Necrophilia Starts	186
Dear Loved Ones	187

Epilogue	193
Proposed Titles for this Book that were Rejected	195
Special Bonus Book Club Discussion Questions	197
Acknowledgements	199
About Dan	201

Preface

I HAVE A CONFESSION. I've never written a book. In fact, my only writing experience consists of bathroom-wall poetry and a series of angry letters to a cereal company.[1] But before you toss this book back into the Barnes & Noble bargain bin next to *Alan Alda's Guide to Backyard Barbecues*, I must point out that I've actually read several books, a few even to completion. And as an accomplished reader, I've walked in the moccasins of the reading public, providing me with a clear edge over the average author who does not read.

What I've also discovered is that while almost anyone can write a book, few people actually should. For writing a book, even a bad one, requires more effort than it's usually worth. Don't get me wrong, writing isn't as hard as working in a steel mill or even selling shoes. But writing is still considered work, especially when you could be watching *Shark Week* instead.

---

1. While a court order restricts me from discussing *McQuinn vs. General Mills*, I'd like to note that the phrase "Cunt Chocula" is now a permanent part of the judicial record of Minnesota's Hennepin County.

Dan McQuinn

Why is writing so hard? Just take a look at the number of words in your average novel. Quite a few, huh? Even if you didn't have to select all the words and arrange them in a meaningful pattern, you would still have a lot of typing. But the hardest part about writing is not what you see but what you don't see. The hardest part is just figuring out what to write about.

The topic of this book did not come easily. I considered many subjects for my first literary endeavor. Given my less-than-torrid writing pace (about a sentence on a good day), I quickly realized that my first book, if ever completed, would most likely be my last. This made my choice of topic all the more important, as having no other meaningful accomplishments, my legacy as a human being was at stake. Hence less weighty ideas, such as *The Giant Book of Fart Jokes*, were put on the back burner (so to speak) to be written in another lifetime. Undeterred, I threw myself at the other extreme and began writing *The Complete Understanding of the Human Brain*, a neurological tour de force that would clarify the inner workings of this misunderstood organ and drive medical innovations for centuries. After a dozen attempts at writing the first chapter, I realized that medical research, especially cranial, is not as simple as it sounds. My exploration would require extensive funding and more than a few non-litigious volunteers. Faced with a publishing deadline,

I decided to leave brain research to the egghead crowd and pieced together what follows, a collection of essays, dialogues, and other attempts at parody that had accumulated on my hard drive over the last few years. Unlike neurological experimentation, this endeavor required little research expense and provided almost zero liability exposure. After all, when was the last time you read a headline that said, "Jury awards $15 million in damages from negligent writer of humorous essays"?

Kids Say the Cutest Things When They're Drunk — A Book of Pointless Satire and Vulgar Humor, Most of It Funny (or *KIDS*, as the biz insiders are calling it) is not an endorsement of underage drinking. For it to be an endorsement, I would have had to accept money, which I have not. But if you are with the powerful child liquor lobby and wish to divert funds from your efforts to introduce malt beverages into school vending machines, or if you are just a teenager in the parking lot of my local liquor store looking to score a sixer, the sponsorship window for the second edition of *KIDS* is still open.

While not advocating alcohol consumption by minors, I recognize that alcohol abuse is not the worst problem facing our youth. Did you know that the average child is almost 2 feet shorter than the average adult? And nearly 100% of all children are infertile and unable to produce their own offspring? And don't even get me started on their inability to puncture a juice box with a straw on their own. Afflicted with such challenges, children, out of anyone, deserve to enjoy an occasional liquid indulgence. And unlike when adults imbibe, we never need to worry about children driving, voting or buying firearms while under the influence. But if the kids do get out of control, well, that's why God invented stun guns.

But I digress, as this book is not about drinking or even cute observations by children. It's not even a real book, lacking a plot, characters or anything resembling a coherent theme. A cynic might say the title is just a shameless ploy to lure you to read further. A cynic would probably also say you have a severe personality disorder for falling for such a ruse. But remember they're the cynic, and therefore they're the one with the personality disorder! Besides, if I were only interested in tricks to grab your attention, I would highlight my story about incest (*Soul Mates*) or my exploration into the origins of necrophilia (*How I Imagine Necrophilia Starts*). And if I really wanted to tease you, I would mention the story about Matt Damon, *People* magazine's Sexiest Man Alive in 2007! (You'll have to find this one on your own!)

So then what is *Kids Say the Cutest Things While They're Drunk* about? I honestly don't know. The title is just one joke of many that I hope you enjoy. Organized loosely around a cradle to grave structure (Spoiler Alert!), each chapter illuminates a different facet of life. I'm told that if you read every other word, you will uncover valuable life lessons and finish in half the time. And if you read it in reverse, you can make yourself think time is traveling backward while missing most of the spelling errors. For maximum enjoyment, though, I encourage you to read all the words and read them in the order that they were written. Only then will you be able to fully experience the rich, subtle nuances of *KIDS* while still getting all the wiener jokes.

If you have not done so already, now is the time to make your purchase, as the Barnes & Noble people are beginning to stare. Take *KIDS* (the book!) home, draw a hot bath, read, laugh and then tell all your friends. Even better, buy multiple copies and give them to your friends! That would make you a great friend, wouldn't it? You will also want to buy extra copies in case you drop any in the bath. This goes for your friends, too.

Enjoy.

Dan McQuinn

Family

Responsibility starts with the parents.

GUIDE TO PARENTING

WHO IS EVER FULLY PREPARED for the experience of raising a child? While animals appear to instinctively know how to raise their young, human beings have yet to evolve to this level. Instead, when faced with the prospect of parenthood, we turn to the usual experts: doctors, scientists and, of course, celebrities. With thousands of books, articles and television shows produced each year focused on the subject of child rearing, prospective parents are left bewildered and confused. For these soon-to-be parents who do not have the time, energy or inclination to consult even a fraction of this information, I've distilled the expert findings into a simple, comprehensive guide — enabling couples to get confused much more efficiently. So if you are tired of hitting the snooze button on your biological clock, the pages that follow will help you assess if you are ready for this awe-inspiring responsibility and provide you with everything you need to know about the joys and horrors of parenthood.

Parental Readiness Test

Give yourself a point for every "yes" answer.

1. Are you old enough to rent a car?
2. Do you have a compatible partner you're willing to stay together with for 35 years for the "sake of the children"?
3. Have you kept a pet alive for more than three weeks?
4. Do you have an endless supply of cash that you have trouble spending on your own?
5. Do you have nothing else interesting to do with your life?
6. Do you enjoy having houseguests who stay for two decades and write on the furniture with magic markers?
7. Subtract a point for every one of the following subversive organizations to which you belong:
   a. The American Nazi Party
   b. NAMBLA
   c. Sam's Club
8. Subtract a point for every one of the following statements you agree with.
   a. Children should be seen and not heard.
   b. Children should be heard and not seen.
   c. Children should be bound and gagged and stuck in the trunk of a Camaro.

9. Subtract a point if you are still living with *your* parents.
10. If you are already pregnant, add 5 points.

SCORING

5 or more — Congratulations! You are ready to be a parent!

2 to 5 — You have parental tendencies but should really live more of your own life before inflicting your value system on another human being.

0 to 2 — You should not consider parenting. If you are lucky, you are gay and can enjoy an active, childless sex life.

Less than 0 — You should not be around children unless under the strict supervision of a law-enforcement official.

Dan McQuinn

Where Do I Get a Child?

Think you know where babies come from? While the days of conceiving your first born in the back seat of a Pontiac Bonneville at the drive-in are becoming a distant memory, parents today have more options than ever for obtaining that son or daughter of their dreams. A few of the more common alternatives:

Conception—The Old-Fashioned Way

Pro: Conception is by far the most enjoyable aspect of raising a child.

Con: Blows out a woman's body like a bag of Jiffy Pop popcorn.

Adoption—Foreign

Pro: Sure-fire way to ensure you have a child who is good at math. When older, can help you fill out your tax return and hook up your Internet connection.

Con: For the rest of your life, may as well wear a sign around your neck that says, "I'm sterile."

Adoption—Domestic

Pro: Best chance to find a child who looks like the rest of your family.

Con: If your child ever strikes it rich or becomes famous, expect visits from a string of hillbilly deadbeats claiming to be true biological parents.

In Vitro Fertilization

Pro: You get to masturbate.

Con: You masturbate already anyway, and with the money for this procedure, you could easily have bought yourself a new SUV.

Surrogate Mother

Pro: Get a child with your genetics while outsourcing the pain and weight gain.

Con: For nine months, it's like having an extra wife you never get to have sex with.

Kidnapping

Pro: You get to pick the child with the features you want who, if you change your mind, you can always return and collect a ransom.

Con: If you get caught, expect to spend the next 20 years sharing a cell with someone who has their own ideas on how to impregnate you.

Dan McQuinn

The Early Years—Decisions, Decisions

Is Home Birth for Me?

For many, hospitals are cold, sterile places for bringing a new being into the world. Sure, the nurses bring you cranberry juice, but with every trip you're running up a mini-bar tab equivalent to the GNP of Scotland.

However, if you are comfortable with the notion of receiving care from a midwife who lacks knowledge of medical techniques developed since the Civil War, a home birth may be for you. Be sure to verify with your insurance company that all expenses will be covered, including carpet stains.

Breast or Bottle?

Breast milk wins hands down. Daddy saves money on formula while Mommy gets big boobs. And it's also healthy for Junior! For the next year, though, expect your house to resemble a National Geographic special.

What's in a Name?

Stick with the basics such as Joe, Bill and Mary. Avoid trendy soap-opera names, as people will assume a child named Brandon or Tiffany is a spoiled, wealthy prick. However, if you are one of the lucky few who can't help but shit cash, ignore this advice, as your child will be a spoiled, wealthy prick anyway.

DIAPERS: PAPER OR PLASTIC?

Unless you are a wealthy prick who can afford a diaper service or, better yet, a nanny, disposable diapers are the only way to go. However, if you are seriously concerned about the environment and are considering using cloth diapers, why are you bringing another life into this world anyway?

POSTPARTUM DEPRESSION: WHY MOMMY GIVES UP SO EARLY?

Most experts agree that postpartum depression can be attributed to a chemical imbalance within a woman's body after childbirth. This extreme form of buyer's remorse can be best treated with more chemicals for the mother and long business trips for the father.

IS YOUR HOUSE BABYPROOF?

Everyone knows that babies love to play with dangerous objects. If you like to keep matches, poison or firearms in your home, you'll need to way to keep these out of babies' prying reach. A good plastic bag should do the trick.

Completely rearranging your life, though, is unnecessary, as infants are so self-absorbed that they are oblivious to your adult activities. Therefore, drug paraphernalia, birth control and pornographic magazines do not have to be hidden—at least until your children are old enough to understand that they need to buy their own.

Dan McQuinn

Should Mommy Work or Stay Home?

Whether a parent should work or stay home with their child is one of the toughest questions most young families face today. The main question a couple must ask themselves is, "Will our child will be better off with a community-college dropout and her ex-con boyfriend as primary caregivers?" If you are like most Americans, the answer is a resounding yes!

If you are one of the lucky ones who can find a community-college dropout willing to spend her day watching music videos with her ex-con boyfriend and your brat, waste no time in securing her services, as finding affordable child care is one of the toughest propositions of parenthood.

If Mommy does stay home, however, don't expect her to ever work again—at least not any type of job that pays a regular salary. Rather, be prepared to fund a series of unsuccessful enterprises that are usually geared to selling bath candles to her stuck-up college friends.

Discipline: To Spank or Not to Spank?

Most experts agree that if you hit your child, you're just teaching them to hit. But the converse is also true. If your child hits you first, you have right to clean his clock. After all, you learned it from him.[1]

---

[1] This tip also works if you are an ex-con hanging out with your girlfriend watching someone else's kids.

School Years

Parent-Teacher Conferences

The most important rule to remember for parent-teacher conferences is to pay attention. Staring at the cleavage of the 22-year-old hottie who is molding the mind of your only descendent will just get you in trouble with both her and your wife. Even if you're not looking at her chest, both she and your wife will assume that's where you're looking and you'll get in trouble. Ah what the hell, take a look. Take a good long look.

Extracurricular Activities

Kids today have an incredible array of ways to spend time after school. Unlike your generation, your children are not limited to watching *Match Game 77* or lighting your neighbor's garbage can on fire. Whether it be drama or intramural fencing, children today can experiment with a wide range of pursuits that will ill-prepare them for the drudgery of their adult working lives.

Driver's Education

One of the first signs of puberty is the incessant demand for a new car. Teens today expect parents to provide them a new automobile as soon as they are eligible for a learner's permit. The teen will resort to every argument imaginable, including peer pressure ("Everyone gets a car nowadays!"), pragmatism ("You won't have to drive me to swim meets anymore") and, in extreme cases, racism ("You would buy me a car if I was an

Inuit!"). Resist all such arguments, as they will ultimately lead to financial ruin and possible loss of human life, unless of course you really hate driving them to their swim meets.

Sex Education

Children are becoming sexually active earlier and earlier. If your children have reached puberty, it's safe to assume they're already having sex, even if they're ugly.

Unless you're ready to raise a grandchild, you must intervene. Sure, you can tell them about safe sex. But will teenagers who forget to close the refrigerator door remember to put on a condom? No, your best bet is to divert their sexual energy. Yes, we're talking about masturbation. With the plethora of titillating stimuli available from the Internet and satellite TV, your youngster never need leave the home, let alone develop a physical relationship with another human being. Just remember to disinfect all household objects before use. Enough said.

Saving for College

While any parent will tell you that college today costs an arm and a leg, experts estimate that by the time a child born today reaches college, tuition for a four-year private university will reach the cost of six arms, four legs, two torsos *and a testicle.* Of course, most respectable universities no longer accept payment in human body parts. But if you do run short of cash, and you will, remember that a healthy human kidney can fetch upwards of $25,000 in certain parts of the world. I'm just saying.

Kids Say the Cutest Things When They're Drunk

CAREER PLANNING

Children are wonderful because they still believe in foolish dreams. But did you know that that these fanciful ideas can actually be a window into your child's future? It turns out that a strong correlation exists between childhood fantasies and what one accomplishes as an adult. So the next time your child tells you what they want to be when they grow up, consult the following guide and discover their real future.

IF YOUR LITTLE BOY WANTS TO:	*HE WILL MOST LIKELY:*
Be a professional athlete.	Be a gym teacher.
Be a doctor.	Be a drug dealer.
Be an astronaut.	Be a shuttle bus driver.
Be a policeman.	Be a security guard.
Be a cowboy.	Be a male prostitute.
Be a spy.	Be a stalker.
Be a garbage man.	Be a garbage man.
Be president of the United States.	Be a convicted felon.
Doesn't know.	Be a guidance counselor.

IF YOUR LITTLE GIRL WANTS TO:	*SHE WILL MOST LIKELY:*
Be a professional athlete.	Be a lesbian gym teacher.
Be a doctor.	Be a nurse.
Be a fashion model.	Be a cashier at Old Navy.
Be a ballerina.	Be a pole dancer.
Be a writer.	Be a remedial English teacher.
Be an actress.	Be a waitress at Applebee's.
Be a princess.	Be a hostess at Applebee's.
Be president of the United States.	Be a dominatrix.
Doesn't know.	Be a housewife.

Adulthood

Congratulations! Your job is almost done. That night you were too lazy to drive to the pharmacy nearly two decades ago is becoming a distant memory, and the bundle of neediness that you subsequently dragged home from the hospital is now ready to leave the nest. It's time to pop the champagne. Your worries are over, right? Well, not exactly. There are still a few concerns you must address:

Your Child's Room

Even if you have no need for the space, redecorate your child's old room as soon as possible. You can turn it into a study, a sewing room or even a setting to display that worthless collection of Princess Diana dinner plates you bought after drinking too much sangria. It doesn't matter what you do with it, just as long as your prodigal child understands that he can't just waltz back to his old room after the first time he loses a job or a relationship goes sour.

Money

Your kids will still need money and will call you for it. In fact, this will be the only reason they will ever call you again. Avoid these calls at all cost. If you find yourself on the phone with one of your kids and you're asked for money, hit the button to play your answering-machine greeting and act confused.

Housekeeping

Now that you no longer have kids living at home, you have no excuse for not cleaning. If you must, hire a maid. It's no time to let everyone figure out that it's *you* who lives like a drunken hobo.

Once you address these final concerns, you're free to throw yourself at all the ambitions and dreams you put on the back burner while raising your children. You now have the time to focus on your life's true calling and start really living. Now, where did those kids leave that remote?

How My Parents Met (As I Imagine)

JACK: Hey, aren't you in my geometry class?

ANN: Why yes. Isn't math fascinating?

JACK: You bet, and it sure is going to help me in my future career selling industrial chemicals to paint manufacturers.

ANN: I noticed you study very hard and always turn your homework assignments in on time. You'll make a great provider for a lucky family someday.

JACK: I like your penmanship.

ANN: Thank you! I have time to practice writing neatly after I clean my room, since television hasn't been invented yet.

JACK: Could I walk you home?

ANN: I wouldn't want to be a bother.

JACK: Nonsense. I have to walk 14 miles to my house, and your house is only nine miles farther. Besides, the heavy snow isn't expected till later.

ANN: Before we get too serious, I just want to let you know that I've never had a boyfriend. Also, I will not have any physical relations with a man until after I'm married, and even then it will be just three times for the sake of having children.

JACK: Great!

Dan McQuinn

Letter from Make-a-Wish

Mr. Daniel McQuinn
403 Hidden Valley Lane
Naperville, IL 60563
March 1, 2011

Dear Mr. McQuinn,

Thank you for contacting the Make-a-Wish Foundation on behalf of your son, Jack. You are correct; we are the group that grants wishes to "retards, palsies and that sort of thing," although we prefer to think of ourselves as the premier wish-granting organization for children.

The Make-a-Wish Foundation is very sorry to hear about your son's condition and wishes him a full recovery. Regrettably, we are unable to grant him a wish at this time. Every year, Make-a-Wish receives thousands of requests for wishes and, unfortunately, funding levels permit us to honor only the requests of the most severe cases. While we are sympathetic to your son's plight, we are only able to grant wishes to children suffering from life-threatening conditions. And while swimmer's ear can be quite painful, the ailment does not qualify under our medical-eligibility rules and, in fact, can usually be treated without even a doctor's visit.

Nevertheless, your wish request intrigued our team enough that making an exception was seriously considered. As I am sure you can imagine, we have to be careful that the wishes granted are fulfilling the dreams of the child and not those of the parent. Ultimately, our board decided that your request was not suitable for an 8-year-old. The decision did not come without regrets, though, as several members of our staff were clearly excited about the idea of planning a Rolling Stones concert at the Playboy mansion.

Besides, Make-A-Wish knows the risks of planning events involving rock and roll singers and our legal department restricts me form commenting on the well-publicized Eric Clapton visit to the Mayo Clinic. Let me just say that the responsibility of safeguarding morphine supplies should always remain with the medical caregiver and *not with a charitable sponsor*.

Finally, we appreciate your generous contribution, but our bank has rejected your check for insufficient funds. In lieu of a personal check, Make-a-Wish does accept donations via cashier's check, money order or a *valid*—key word here—credit card from any of the major credit card companies.

Dan McQuinn

Thanks again for your interest in Make-a-Wish. Should your son contract a more serious condition such as leukemia or a spinal injury, we will reconsider your application. Good Luck! There's always hope.

Sincerely,

Vincent Williams
Midwest Region Wish Coordinator
Make-a-Wish Foundation of America

WHEN MAKE-A-WISH GOES BAD

— Mommy, this isn't the usual route to the hospital.
— We're not going to the hospital today.
— But what about my treatments?
— Dr. Robinson said it would be OK if you miss one day.
— But where are we going?
— You'll see.
— Hey, there's the stadium where the Colts play. Why are you pulling in the parking lot? There's no game today.
— I said you'll see.
— There's some of the Colts holding a sign and balloons. Is that Peyton Manning?
— It sure is.
— "Welcome Tommy" ... All of this is for me?
— That's right. It's a Make-a-Wish. Are you surprised?
— Oh my fucking God! I'm dying! I knew it. I'm fucking dying!

Divorce

DAD: Jimmy, your mother and I need to talk to you.

SON: I'm not in trouble, am I?

MOM: No, no. (laughing) You're not in trouble.

DAD: We just have something important we need to discuss.

MOM: First of all, we both want to let you know that we love you very much.

DAD: And more than anything we want you to be happy.

SON: I am happy.

DAD: Good, because your mother and I are getting a divorce.

SON: A divorce? Don't you love each other?

MOM: We love each other very much.

DAD: We even tried several counselors and they all came to the same conclusion.

Mom: It's you.

Son: Me?

Mom: You see, your father and I always imagined that any child of ours would be more like us—you know, cool.

Dad: But when you came along, you were so well mannered and studied all the time—

Mom: What your father is trying to say is that you're a dork.

Son: A dork?

Dad: Yeah! That's the word I was looking for. A dork, a great big dork.

Mom: Don't worry. We still love you. We just can't stand being with you.

Son: But you always said to study hard and be a good listener.

Mom: We're supposed to say that. We're the parents.

Dad: We thought you'd rebel at least a little.

Mom: Grow some balls.

Dad: At first we thought we could put you up for adoption.

Mom: But we got no takers.

Dan McQuinn

DAD: We learned that a dorky child is a real deal-breaker.

SON: I can't believe this.

MOM: But finally your father and I realized that if you were adopted by someone else, we'd lose you as a tax deduction.

DAD: If we get divorced, we each only have to see you half the time and we still get to keep you as a deduction.

MOM: We get to write you off and still be able to write you off!

(Both laugh)

SON: If I'm a dork, it's your fault. You gave me a chemistry set in kindergarten.

DAD: That was a bong!

SON: Fine. If you don't wan to to live with me, I'll live with Uncle Gary!

(STORMS OUT)

MOM: OK, but he doesn't get your tax deduction.

DAD: Or your chemistry set!

MOM: Uncle Gary ...

MOM & DAD: (together) What a dork!

EDUCATION

WHERE IGNORANCE IS LEARNED.

First Job

When I started kindergarten, my mom told me school was necessary in order to get a job when I was older. After my first day of school, this is how I imagined a typical job interview.

INTERVIEWER: From your resume here, it shows that you can color within the lines and know how to use scissors?

ME: I can also be quiet during fire drills!

INTERVIEWER: Impressive. But do you have any finger-painting experience?

ME: In fact, I just finished this one. I call it *Dog Sniffing a Daisy*.

INTERVIEWER: Very nice.

ME: And I was the first one in my class to finish!

INTERVIEWER: It's clear that you're a fit for our needs. I'm just going to cut to the chase. We have an entry-level finger-painting position open, with excellent opportunities for advancement. I can start you at $90,000 with full benefits and a 20 percent bonus.

Me: I like finger-painting, but I also like recess. Do you have jobs playing recess?

Interviewer: Usually, we fill our recess positions internally. You could, though, start in finger-painting and move into recess down the road.

Me: Mmm ... I'll have to think about it.

SEVEN HABITS OF HIGHLY EFFECTIVE THIRD-GRADE BOYS

1. Be persistent. *No* means "Keep whining and you'll eventually get what you want."
2. Think "winner takes all." Sharing is for second-graders.
3. Seek first to avoid blame and then blame someone else.
4. Always take rock. Paper can cover a rock, but paper tears and rocks hurt.
5. If you see shadows in your bedroom, they must be trying to kill you.
6. Avoid time-wasters such as naps and showers.
7. Sharpen the pencil. When wrestling your sister for the TV remote, a freshly sharpened pencil can mean the difference between *Spiderman* and the *Dora the Explorer* marathon.

Morning Visitor

Mr. Harty: Ok, class it's now time to read some of the haikus you've been working on. Let's see, the first one I have here is by Danny and is titled *Morning Visitor*.

Danny: I didn't think these would be read aloud.

Mr. Harty: It starts, "Gently waits alone." Obviously, this is written by someone who has problems socializing and suffers painful loneliness.

Danny: Oh, my God.

Mr. Harty: Yes. A social outcast, extremely unpopular, someone so uncomfortable in his own skin that he is afraid to speak up.

Danny: But—

Mr. Harty: Yet he is waiting ... for someone? Perhaps his morning visitor? A secret lover? It's all so cloak-and-dagger ... like an unexpressed homosexual desire.

Danny: I'm not gay.

Mr. Harty: "Soon to be gone forever."

Mr. Harty: Possibly a reference to the AIDS virus or feelings of suicide due to his filthy, forbidden lifestyle.

Danny: I'm going to kill myself.

Mr. Harty: But wait, he finishes with, "Dew on my window." I think we all know where he's going with this *moist climax*.

Danny: He better not read *Afternoon Delight*.

Romeo and Juliet Essay Questions

1. How did Shakespeare view love and death? Does all true love have to die? Is it ever acceptable to love a dead person? Frame your response in terms of legal, moral and hygienic considerations.

2. How do the suicidal impulses exhibited by Romeo and Juliet compare with your own feelings? Have you ever wanted something so badly you felt like killing yourself? What stopped you? How would you overcome such obstacles in the future?

3. Why did Juliet put so much faith in Friar Lawrence? Have you ever trusted a clergy member who gave you bad advice? Or gave you a drug that made you drowsy? Describe in detail, including any feelings of shame or embarrassment.

4. Explore Shakespeare's use of fate as a theme. Were the "star-crossed lovers" destined to self-destruction? Is a predestined life worth living? Prove the existence of fate, showing all your work. Do the same for random chance and free will.

Kids Say the Cutest Things When They're Drunk

5. Explain the relationship between parents and children in *Romeo and Juliet*. Wouldn't everything be easier if parents did not exist at all? Provide examples of how eliminating your parents would improve your own life. Extra credit if you are an actual orphan.
6. Compare and contrast the use of light and dark imagery in *Romeo and Juliet* with Herman Melville's *Moby Dick*. Do you think Romeo would still love Julia if she were a whale? What if it were dark?
7. What role does Mercutio play in the life of Romeo? Do you have a friend of the same sex for whom you have confusing feelings? Are either of you prone to violent outbursts? Describe any homoerotic dreams you may have experienced, noting dominant and submissive roles.
8. In *Romeo and Juliet*, Shakespeare makes use of the English language to convey his tale. Describe how words and punctuation can be arranged to express ideas and tell stories. Now do the same exercise without words.
9. Select one line from *Romeo and Juliet* and show how these words have affected the development of 20th century agricultural policies. Incorporate concepts such as the rise of socialism and the use of iambic pentameter.

10. Imagine you can travel in time back to the age of Shakespeare. Now imagine that you are trapped and cannot get back. Did you remember to bring toothpaste? Deodorant? Describe what it feels like living your remaining days trying to ensure that you will be born again by not altering history. Now do the same without running water.

A Very Brief History of Time

10000 B.C. Early Cro-Magnons first to mark time using bodily functions. First utterance of "See you in two shakes."

4000 B.C. Stonehenge created. Believed to be either one of the first ancient timepieces or the earliest known British dental records.

1500 B.C. Ancient Egyptians pioneer use of sundial. Concept of saving time proliferates, spurring widespread adoption of slavery.

45 B.C. Julius Caesar institutes Julian calendar, vowing never to miss an orgy again.

0 A.D. Transition to counting time forward results in most famous hotel-reservations foul-up ever and humanity's savior spends his first night in a barn.

1582	Pope Gregory XIII replaces Julian calendar with more accurate Gregorian calendar. To synchronize on new calendar, two whole weeks are skipped. Widely heralded by common man as "two less weeks of misery and filth."
1881	At the decree of American President James Garfield, Gregorian calendar replaced by Garfield calendar.
1884	Advent of transcontinental railroads forces adoption of standard time zones to curtail advent of transcontinental train wrecks.
1916	Germany adopts daylight-saving time to lengthen the working day, allowing more time for futile trench warfare.
1920	Einstein's Theory of Relativity postulates how time is relative, explaining how the passage of time actually slows when being visited by one's relatives.
1970	First electronic digital watch provides easy way for females to identify unsuitable sexual partners.
1983	First Swatch provides easy way for homosexuals to identify unsuitable sexual partners.

1990   Hammer Time.

2000   Mass disappointment when computer calendar software does not destroy the world.

2008   Stephen Hawking releases an updated version of *A Brief History of Time.* Widely criticized for lack of wacky "History of Time" timeline.

Dan McQuinn

Take Our Daughters to Work Day

On April 28, 2011 my daughter accompanied me to my place of employment as part of the National Take Our Daughters to Work Day program. Below is the report she submitted to her school.

My Dad's Job
By Rosie McQuinn

8:15 A.M.

We prepare to leave our home for the journey to my dad's office.

My dad is a marketing manager for a company that makes plastic washers for screws and other things that I would not understand. His company does not call the washers plastic, though, as that would make them sound cheap. Instead, they are referred to as "non-metallic." Companies that make metallic washers are run by bad people, because their washers are cheap and ruin something called margins.

My dad's job is very important because these washers "would not sell themselves" and we would be stuck in a world held together by cheap, metallic washers.

We are running late because Dad cannot find his favorite coffee cup.

8:25 A.M.

Found it! Apparently, someone hid it in the cabinet with the other coffee cups.

8:30 A.M.

Still have not left house because Dad spilled coffee on the cat.

8:40 A.M.

On the road at last! Normally, I would be finishing language arts at this time. I don't miss language arts.

9:05 A.M.

As we drive, Dad warns me about misbehaving at his work. Also, I can't say anything about the office supplies he sells on eBay.

9:20 A.M.

While changing lanes, Dad cuts off another driver and nearly swerves into a cement truck. Dad is then pulled over and issued a ticket for failing to yield and driving without an insurance card. Although I think the hand gestures he exchanged with the other driver may have had something to do with it. How could he have known that he was an off-duty policeman?

9:45 A.M.

We arrive at my dad's office and enter through the back door. I soon realize that I am the only kid here. Apparently, Take Your Daughters to Work Day is next week. I hope I don't get too behind on my homework. Come to think of it, I also had a test today.

9:55 A.M.

We go the break area and Dad gets another cup of coffee. Fortunately, no cats are near. He then talks to a man with a big belly about how the Cubs need to fix their bullpen.

10:15 A.M.

The conversation shifts from the Cubs bullpen to how their accounting department has a pony! Her name is Kelli and she is very pretty. Everyone wants to ride her.

10:25 A.M.

My dad and the man with the big belly are now talking about how they are the only two people who get any work

Kids Say the Cutest Things When They're Drunk

done at their company until a man with a nice sweater enters and the talking stops. I learn later that this is the boss. He seems so much younger than my dad. Dad says he could have been the boss but he does not like to play politics. My dad does not like to play many games, except for those on the scratch-off lottery tickets.

Dad asks his boss if he has seen the baseball game, but his boss only scowls. My dad says his boss would be less cranky if he had a girlfriend.

10:30 A.M.

We walk past fancy offices with wood where the "hotshots" sit on our way to my dad's cubicle. Dad prefers his office because it is where all the real work happens, and it is near the bathroom. My dad, though, doesn't like his cubemate, Glen. Glen has bad acne and talks a lot about his GPS system. Glen is out sick today, so I can sit in his chair. His desk smells like rotting meat. While my dad starts up his computer, he lets me rummage through Glen's drawers and play with his hole puncher.

10:40 A.M.

Dad is laughing at an e-mail. He will not tell me what he is laughing at, but I think it involves a picture of a woman peeing on a man's face.

10:42 A.M.

Dad tries to print the picture on the printer in the hallway, but the printer jams. My dad looks worried.

10:45 A.M.

Unable to fix the printer, we leave.

11:00 A.M.

Back at his cubicle, Dad works at his computer. He tells me he is designing a new promotion, although it looks a lot like playing solitaire. I find a stack of Glen's business cards and begin punching holes.

11:25 A.M.

Lunchtime! We eat at the company cafeteria. Dad says eating here will make me appreciate Mom's cooking. He has a meatloaf sandwich, while I try the fish sticks. A lady with flowers on her blouse stops to say hello. She asks me if I just started working at their company. This is the fourth person to ask me this question today, but we laugh anyway.

When she leaves, Dad tells me that the woman we just met wants to have babies with him. I am not to say anything to Mom about this, though.

1:15 P.M.

I get to attend an important business meeting. For the first 10 minutes, we discuss the poor quality of the cafeteria food. A man with heavy cologne asks me if I liked my fish sticks.

1:25 P.M.

Not everyone is here yet, but it is decided to start the meeting anyway.

The cologne guy then makes a presentation on how sales are way down and everyone needs to FOCUS! For the next 10 minutes, we discuss how the Cubs suck at focus.

The cologne guy then makes a joke at the expense of manufacturing. Everyone agrees. They're idiots!

A man with a foreign accent then goes on about how the competition is kicking their butts. He says we need to be more like the Dallas Cowboys. (Even I know the Cowboys now suck, and I'm a girl!) He will not stop talking, and everyone looks bored. I'm beginning to wish I hadn't had the fish sticks.

2:15 P.M.

My dad's boss enters, and the man in the red shirt finally stops talking. My dad's boss is mad that some idiot jammed the printer while wasting company resources.

This is when I threw up.

2:17 P.M.

Meeting adjourned.

2:20 P.M.

A janitor comes to clean up the mess I made. He does not look happy. Dad tells his boss that he should probably take me home and he'll work the rest of the day from our house.

3:15 P.M.

We arrive home and Dad plays with my brother's Playstation®3 until dinnertime. After dinner, my dad logs into eBay and gets eight dollars for Glen's hole puncher.

I learned a lot going to my dad's work. I especially learned that I don't want to work at a company that makes non-metallic washers. I still think I would rather be a movie actress or someone who watches other people's dogs. I think everyone should go to their dad's work. I would recommend, though, bringing your own lunch or at least not ordering the fish sticks.

HIGHLY RECOMMENDED

Johns Hopkins University
Office of Admissions
Johns Hopkins University
Mason Hall
3400 N. Charles St.
Baltimore, MD 21218-2683

Dec. 1, 2010

To Whom It May Concern,

It is my honor to recommend Garrett Simpson for admission to the Johns Hopkins University pre-med program. For the last four years, I had the pleasure to know and work with Garrett in my role as guidance counselor at St. Bartholomew Catholic Boys School. I hope my perspective will be helpful in your evaluation of this exceptional candidate.

My first contact with Garrett was in the fall of 2007 when he organized the school blood drive. His creative ideas attracted new donors and catapulted the drive to become the most successful in school history. Garrett's resourcefulness was duly recognized and he became the youngest student ever to be awarded the school's "Monster Vein" award, although the Red Cross would later reject a portion of the donations for being of canine origin.

Emboldened by success, Garrett challenged himself to find additional ways to give back to the community, including donating time to help a local scout troop earn their merit badge in taxidermy. He also entertained residents at an adult care center, delighting patients with hand-puppet shows in what often turned out to be their last moments on earth. Earning the nickname "God's Warm-up Act," Garrett's nursing-home performances had an eerie timeliness, as at least one patient would invariably pass on during each of his visits. Accidental suffocation was the usual cause of death, but in one incident the body of a 27-year-old orderly was also discovered, the apparent victim of a scissors mishap. Nevertheless, all could take solace in knowing that their last hours were filled with joy and amusement—thanks to this special young man.

Touching lives is what Garrett Simpson is all about. It's rare that one encounters a person who affects so many and even rarer that this person is still in high school. I feel honored and blessed knowing Garrett, and I am sure Johns Hopkins will feel the same.

I would be remiss, though, if I did not comment on Garrett's extraordinary academic accomplishments. With an inquisitive nature and a passion for learning, Garrett excelled at all subjects but particularly shined when it came to the sciences. With a keen interest in physiology, Garrett spent much time in the sophomore biology lab testing the impact of forces on the body. His series of squirrel-drop experiments provided a rich body of data for understanding trauma in small mammals, as well as brilliant classroom entertainment.

Garrett's true depth of character, though, came to light in his junior year when he confronted a series of personal tragedies that no person at any age should face. The first incident involved his older sister, Rachel, who fell down a flight of stairs while trying to hang a family portrait. Under normal circumstances, she might have survived, but the hammer she had been holding slipped from her hands and broke her fall at the base of the stairs—and the base of her skull.

To cope with the unexpected tragedy, Garrett and his parents took a trip to their country cottage a few weeks after the funeral. Seeking to relax with a weekend of fishing and fresh air, the family hoped the getaway would provide them a chance to begin healing. While details of the weekend are murky, one fact is painfully clear: Misfortune struck again, and Garrett returned home an orphan.

Authorities are unclear on what caused the Simpson rowboat to capsize and even less clear why his parents were unable to survive a spill into water only 4 feet deep. Garrett, who at the time of the accident was reportedly alone on shore, believes a wayward goose may have been responsible.

Now living with an aunt, Garrett has not let these tragedies stop his career aspirations. In fact, he appears more determined than ever to gain admission to Johns Hopkins and pursue a dual degree in toxicology and forensics. According to a modest Garrett, he seeks "the most efficient way to impact the most people."

I recommend Garrett to your program with absolute confidence. At St. Bartholomew, Garrett left an indelible mark in the minds of the faculty (as well as the floor of the biology lab), and we expect great things from him in the years ahead. Knowing Garrett, he will not disappoint.

Thank you once again for the opportunity to highly recommend such a special and impressive young man.

Sincerely,

Jeff Golding
Senior Guidance Counselor
St. Bartholomew H.S.
Oak Lawn, IL

BIOLOGY

WHEN NOBODY ELSE WILL LOVE YOU, LOVE YOURSELF.

WHEN I FIRST LEARNED WHERE BABIES COME FROM

— So there's no stork?

— And a woman's body has a hole?

— And the man puts his wiener in the hole.

— And it's kind of like peeing, but it's not.

— And the baby comes out of this same hole?

— And Mom and Dad did this?

— Now I know you're fucking with me.

— The F-word means what?

Dan McQuinn

A Conversation between the Two Cutest Girls on the High School Bus (As I Imagine)

BLONDE: Do you see that cute guy with the windbreaker?

BRUNETTE: You mean the one who we quickly turn away from whenever he looks in our direction?

BLONDE: Yeah, that's him.

BRUNETTE: I think his name is Dan. My brother is in his algebra class and says that once you get to know him, he's really cool.

BLONDE: I wish I had the guts to talk to him. But whenever I'm near him I get all flustered and can't think of anything to say.

BRUNETTE: I hear he's very funny and does a killer impersonation of all the Sweathogs.

BLONDE: Wow! It must be great to have talent.

BRUNETTE: He's also the quickest in his class at solving polynomial equations. He's not just book smart, though. My brother also says Dan always gets the high score on the

Space Invaders but never enters his initials because he's so modest.

BLONDE: That's so cool!

BLONDE: Yeah, with his brains and eye-hand coordination, he's probably going to be a surgeon or an astronaut.

BRUNETTE: He could even become an international rock star. Can you imagine being Mrs. Astronaut or Mrs. International Rock Star?

BLONDE: Stop that!

BRUNETTE: I bet you he's really good at sex, too.

BLONDE: How would you know?

BRUNETTE: Just look at the way he carries himself. How many kids have the guts to do their homework on the bus? He just doesn't care what others think. What a rebel! You really should ask him out.

BLONDE: Aren't you forgetting about Josh?

BRUNETTE: Oh, that's right. What are you going to do?

BLONDE: When Josh and I first started dating, it was great, but ever since he became the team captain, all he cares about is stupid football. But looking at Dan every day, I realize how boring and shallow Josh really is.

BRUNETTE: It's not even a fair comparison.

BRUNETTE: Why don't you just dump Josh then and ask Dan out?

BLONDE: He would never go out with me.

BRUNETTE: What are you talking about? You're one of the cutest girls in the school!

BLONDE: I'm sure he's already dating somebody—probably a college girl or a stewardess.

BRUNETTE: Shhh! Here he comes!

BLONDE: Oh my God!

BRUNETTE: Are those new shoes?

BLONDE: Oh these? I just found them in the closet.

BRUNETTE: They're so cute!

BLONDE: (whispers) Is he gone?

BRUNETTE: It's safe. Now he's trying to untangle his backpack from his orthodontic headgear.

BLONDE: He's going to have such great teeth.

BRUNETTE: Mrs. Perfect Smile!

BLONDE: (sighs) We'd make such great babies together.

GONE FISHING

I HAVE A SECRET THAT I'm embarrassed to talk about. It involves something that I like to do that many people find dirty. I haven't told anyone about it, and if I don't tell somebody soon, I feel like I'm going to burst! If let you in on my secret, can you promise not to tell anyone?

OK, then, here we go—I like fishing. I like fishing a lot! I only started fishing recently. I can't believe what I was missing! For starters, fishing feels so good, like nothing else in this world. And best of all, I can do it all by myself. In fact, I prefer to fish alone. That's why I do most of my fishing at night and have become really good at fishing in the dark. I've also found that if I wake up early, I can fish in the morning, too! And sometimes during the day, if nobody is around, I can sneak in even more fishing!

The first time I got a bite I was so excited I screamed. Now when I fish, I try to keep quiet so I do not disturb anyone. Fishing is so relaxing. After a night of fishing, I sleep like a city worker.

When I'm not fishing, I like to think about fishing and plan my next fishing session. Proper preparation is key. Choice of lure is especially important, as you will never get a bite without good visual stimulation. While I like lures that are pretty and flashy, the best ones are those that are the most lifelike. I like to spice it up by trying different lures and even different colors! When all else fails, though, I have my go-to favorites that always provide me complete satisfaction.

Of course, care for my rod and reel is also very important. I like to keep a small towel handy to keep my pole clean. You don't necessarily need a towel. A tissue or even an old shirt will do as long as it's soft. Trust me. I know, as I have tried almost everything in the house—even lunch meat! Talk about spicing it up! I would not recommend lunch meat, though, as it breaks easily when rubbed, and the smell doesn't go away.

Sometimes the urge to fish hits me when I least expect it, such as while I'm riding the bus or sitting in algebra class. I never fish at school or even talk about it, as my classmates would make fun of me. Girls especially find fishing icky, especially the part about touching the worm. If they only knew how to do it, though, I think they would like fishing, too.

Believe it or not, for all the time I spend fishing, I've never caught a real fish! I like to imagine what it would be like to catch a real one. I would be so excited I would tell everyone I know, even the kids at school. Of course, I would be gentle and try not to hurt the fish. I definitely would not eat it. Now, that would be icky!

Fishing is the best, but I'm worried. I'm afraid I may be fishing too much. All I can think about is fishing, and I wonder if I am turning into some kind of fishing weirdo. Sometimes I fish so much that my wrists get sore and I get blisters from grabbing my pole so hard. Do you think I take a break? Not me. I just rub on some lotion and start casting again.

With all this talk about fishing, I am finding it hard to concentrate. All I can think about is—that's right—fishing! I am going to need to take a break. I feel so much better, though, having told you about my *dirty* habit, I don't think I need to keep it a secret anymore. If anyone asks, just tell them I've gone fishing!

Dan McQuinn

FIRST-DATE CRIB NOTES

He	*She*
Talk slowly and confidently with the steely demeanor of a stallion.	Playfully toss hair with the grace of a riding pony.
Find common ground. Tell her how you hate racism and ATM fees.	Find common ground. Tell him how you hate crunchy peanut butter and ATM fees.
Be sure to let her know that you've been to Europe, but do not mention that you went with your parents.	Be sure to let him know that you've been to Europe, but do not mention that you went with your ex-boyfriend.
If asked what you do, say you work in commodities. Under no circumstances should you mention the produce section at Safeway.	Ask probing questions that will allow you to estimate his net worth and future earnings potential. Be subtle. Avoid direct questions such as "What is your net worth and future earnings potential?"
Imagine what kind of underwear she is wearing, with an eye toward signs of sexual permissiveness. Note: If too permissive, could be a prostitute.	Imagine what he would look like in a wedding tuxedo, with an eye toward signs of style and taste. Note: If too much style and taste, could be gay.

He	**She**
Avoid talking about "the rash."	Avoid talking about "the rash."
Look for visual clues of interest. Does body language say, "Smother me with kisses"? Or "Smother me with a pillow if this conversation lasts a minute longer"?	Remember not to yawn, as it makes you look fat. Also, show cleavage! Do we even have to write this one down?
In case of a conversational lull, remember you always kill with the Monty Python dead-parrot sketch.	In case of a conversational lull, probe further on his earnings potential.
Under no circumstances should you mention Albert Pujols' slugging percentage, Sonic Mario or your fascination with *iCarly*.	Under no circumstances should you mention your mother, your medications or how you met your last boyfriend at the abortion clinic.
And definitely do not tell her that you have nicknamed your penis Elmer Fudd.	And definitely do not tell him that your vagina has been nicknamed Pepé Le Pew.
Figure out a playful way to bring up the topic of sex. Maybe start with a discussion of animal husbandry?	If he starts talking about weird topics such as animal husbandry, get away as fast as possible.

Dan McQuinn

WHEN I FIRST REALIZED I NEEDED TO FIND A NEW COLLEGE ROOMMATE

— Hey, dude, how about we play some quarters?

— With just the two of us?

— Sure. We'll get drunk quicker!

—- I don't know. I really should be studying for my midterm.

— It's only a midterm. It's not like it's a final.

— Good point. I'll get the beer.

— OK. Here are the rules. We take turns trying to bounce a quarter into a glass. If you miss, you drink. If you make it, your opponent must drink. If you point with your finger, though, you drink as well.

— There's just the two of us. Why would I be pointing?

— Then you have nothing to worry about. OK, and if you say "drink," "drank" or "drunk," you need to remove an article of clothing.

— Isn't that a little weird?

— I always play this way. It just makes it a little more interesting.

— If there were girls here, maybe, but I don't know.

— Fine. You don't have to go any further than your underpants. And if a quarter falls on the floor, you need to stick your tongue into the ear of the person next to you.

— But that would be you!

— And if I drop a quarter, I'll have to stick my tongue in your ear.

— That does not make me feel any better.

— OK. The last rule is no proper names.

— And what happens if a player says a proper name?

— The other player gets to punish him ... in the manner of his choosing.

— I really need a drink now.

— Uh-oh, you said "drink" ...

Dan McQuinn

SOUL MATES

How many men can honestly say that the woman they choose to marry is their true soul mate?

I can.

The bond between Goldie and me goes beyond that of husband and wife. As the song says, we're lovers and we're best friends. We do everything together. We watch the same TV shows, laugh at the same jokes—my gosh, we even sometimes wear the same clothes!

And it doesn't stop with shared interests. Goldie has blond hair and green eyes. I have blond hair and green eyes. Goldie can wiggle her ears. I can wiggle my ears. Goldie's middle toe is longer than her other toes. Yep, you guessed it—my middle toe is longer than my other toes. It's as if a cosmic force created us especially for each other.

But my love for Goldie goes beyond physical similarities. I love her inner beauty, the beauty she shows me daily as a loving wife and the mother of our four wonderful children. She puts her heart into everything she does, and it shows.

So you may ask, "How does one find such a perfect mate?" In my case, I only had to look as far as my own backyard.

Kids Say the Cutest Things When They're Drunk

You see, Goldie and I are childhood sweethearts. Her family, the Hendersons, have been living next door to our family since before either of us was even born!

As a boy, I was always smitten with Goldie. You would think I would have preferred the company of other boys, but from the earliest age I could never get enough of the girl with the yellow braids next door. My dad would say we were like two peas in a pod. And if he was drinking, he would always substitute the word *pot* for *pod*, adding, "Now, that doesn't mean you two can pee in the same pot together!"

While we didn't pee in the same pot, we did have sleepovers, usually after one of Mrs. Henderson's impromptu daiquiri parties that for some reason happened only when Mr. Henderson was out of town. These parties always ended the same way, with my mom falling asleep on a lawn chair and my dad pulling Goldie and me off the Henderson trampoline. He would then carry us to the floor of the Henderson den, where he and Mrs. Henderson would tuck Goldie and me into our matching Princess Lea and Luke Skywalker sleeping bags.

Of course, we could never sleep, and neither could my dad or Mrs. Henderson, who we would hear giggling through the night. Sometimes, my dad would make her laugh so hard that she would scream!

It was at moments like this that Goldie and I talked about our future. She would always want to be the next

Marie Osmond, and I naturally dreamed of being the next Donnie. We loved to sing own version of *A Little Bit Country, a Little Bit Rock 'n' Roll*, which invariably would provoke a "Pipe down you kids!" from my dad as he fumbled through the kitchen drawers looking for a fresh pack of Mr. Henderson's cigarettes.

Years later, my dad would look back fondly on the time spent with the Hendersons as the best years of his life. Curiously, in almost the same breath, he would also warn me never to date the girl next door, and for a short time after his death I honored those wishes. But I never could understand his reasons, and not only did I date the girl next door but I ultimately married her!

It's hard to believe that Goldie and I now have our own children. What's even more amazing is the job Goldie has done raising our crew, especially with their special needs. While most women would collapse under the burden of raising four children born without armpits, Goldie relishes every moment. And when she says, "Let's have one more," I know she is not kidding.

Although our children more resemble Mr. Roboto than either Donnie or Marie, they all love to sing just like their parents. And while we will probably never get our own television show, Goldie and I have become closer than ever as our family has grown, and Goldie and I have become *more than soul mates*.

CHRISTMAS

CHRISTMAS IS NO HOLIDAY.

Here Comes Santa Claus

Mom: Shhh! You'll wake Danny.

Dad: You didn't seem to care about that last night, heh heh.

Mom: (glares) Just keep wrapping.

Dad: But I think he knows already.

Mom: Why? Did you tell him?

Dad: No, of course not. It's just that when we saw Santa at the mall, he said the beard looked fake, and he wondered how Santa could be in so many stores at the same time.

Mom: Well, what did you say?

Dad: I told him Santa was really the Dark Prince and he inhabits the bodies of fat old men around the world in exchange for their souls. What else could I say?

Mom: You didn't!

Dad: Of course not. I used the old "He's one of Santa's helpers" line.

Mom: Do you think he believed you?

Dad: It seemed to satisfy him, but I can't be too sure.

Mom: They're little for only so long ...

(The next morning)

DANNY: How did Santa know I needed a new coffee cup? I can't wait to show the guys at the office ...

GREETINGS FROM THE MCQUINNS

Greetings from the McQuinns

This past year has been a banner year for the McQuinn household. While America was fighting two wars and an unprecedented economic collapse, we were waging a war on calories. If my waistline is any indication, Baskin-Robbins has proved to be a much bigger menace than Osama Bin Laden. Hey, do we still need to be afraid of this guy? I'm not saying we should stop looking for this slippery character, but I think most Americans would agree that Lindsay Lohan now poses a bigger threat.

Closer to home, our Rose began first grade, joined Girl Scouts and started wearing lipstick! The year of firsts was capped with her theatrical debut as the Virgin Mary in her class Christmas pageant. At least we know she didn't land this role via the casting couch!

Not to be outdone, our little Jack entered preschool, where he blossomed from a shy 3-year old into a boisterous 4-year-old who "disrupts the learning experience of his classmates." Way to go, Jack!

Dan McQuinn

While my job continued to be joyless and unrewarding, Barb delayed my retirement dreams further by persisting to be a stay-at-home mom. All kidding aside, her day is full of valuable and important activities that I'm sure we've discussed but currently elude me.

And who could forget Corky? We do all the time. Where is it written that a dog needs to be fed every day?

And no McQuinn Christmas letter would be considered complete without a report on our annual family excursion. Every year we explore another exotic part of the tri-state area, and this year's trip to Milwaukee was no exception. Can you imagine our delight when we discovered the free-samples policy on what would be the first of multiple brewery tours? And we all howled when little Jack chided the barmaid for serving us "piss water." Kids say the cutest things when they're drunk.

The year is ending on a sad note as Grandma Claire continues her battle with cancer (stomach???). In spite of being 85 and bedridden, she has not mellowed and still curses like a union foreman. And the kids are getting a rare front-row view of a loved one being eaten alive by a fatal disease. Thank you, Grandma Claire!

Barb is calling me now, so it's time to wrap up. She's helping Rose earn a scouting badge by organizing a holiday-season food drive. Apparently, they need my help removing expiration labels from the packets of meat they found at the back of our refrigerator. On this charitable note, I wish season's tidings to you and yours!

The McQuinns

Dan, Barb, Rose, Jack & Corky

Yankee Swap

Jeanine, Dan's co-worker:

It was just supposed to be fun, you know, a way to share some holiday spirit with your co-workers.

Rita, office secretary:

He was all excited at first and as usual appointed himself in charge. Of course, he had a long list of rules that only he could follow.

Mrs. McQuinn, Dan's mother:

We don't do gift exchanges anymore.

Tom, Dan's cubicle partner:

We all just played along, except for Ralph, who kept asking stupid questions, trying to mess him up and shit.

Tina, Ralph's ex-wife:

When he sets his mind to it, Ralph can be a real prick.

Wade, Ralph's lunch buddy:

When Ralph asked if all the wrapping paper was hypoallergenic, I almost peed in my pants!

MARK, IT SUPPORT:

Nothing was supposed to be more than $15, but all gifts had to be at least $10.

EVAN, PURCHASING:

We weren't supposed to use gift cards either, but most of us just bought gift cards. What else can you get someone for less than $15?

BETH, INTERN:

Things were going smoothly at first, but you could see Dan getting agitated the longer his present did not get picked. It became kind of a game for everyone not to pick his gift.

PHYLLIS, TED'S SECRETARY:

Dan started criticizing the other gifts, real shitty and all.

TED, DAN'S SUPERVISOR:

Since we're on work premises, we can't have alcohol. But I gave one of those *Wine Drinking for Dummies* books with a corkscrew—it cost more than $15—but Dan said it was provincial.

KAREN, BETH'S MENTOR:

Beth finally opened Dan's present and shrieked. There were two hamsters with little stocking caps, like you see on elves. He must have sewed them himself.

Dan McQuinn

Kevin, shipping clerk:

I don't know if he intended those hamsters to be dead or not, but either way, not cool.

Tom, Dan's neighbor:

He's got a robotic Santa he sets up in his garage in September, and one year he even had a real reindeer in his backyard. He's really into Christmas.

Raymond, building custodian:

The ladies didn't want me to put the hamsters in the garbage, so we have this heavy-duty shredder ...

Larry, engineering:

Everyone started laying into Dan, especially Ralph.

Sonya, human resources:

He just got hurt and defensive. He even had tears in his eyes.

Jim, Dan's younger brother:

He's such a pussy.

Darren, Ralph's supervisor:

Ralph wouldn't let up. He called Dan a crazy fuck and said he needs therapy. The next thing you know, Dan's got the corkscrew and he's lunging at Ralph's neck!

DALE, HUMAN RESOURCES DIRECTOR:

Fortunately, one of the younger guys was able to grab his arm and twist it behind his back à la Chuck Norris. Dan dropped the corkscrew, but not before tearing a big hole in Ralph's shirt.

VALERIE, ACCOUNTING:

He mumbled a halfhearted apology and sat down. I thought someone would have called the police, but we just resumed exchanging gifts, in complete silence.

RALPH, CONTRACT EMPLOYEE:

What an asshole! They'll be hearing from my attorney.

RHONDA, MARKETING:

Next year we're going back to Secret Santas.

Dan McQuinn

Frugal Christmas Ideas

1. Instead of buying Christmas cards, make your own! With a pair of scissors, construction paper and a stack of old magazines, you can create distinctive cards with the look and feel of a personalized ransom note. And don't forget that by hand-delivering, you can both save on postage and avoid being traced by the authorities!

2. When buying Christmas decorations, the earlier the better. Everyone knows that January is the best month for bargains, but did you know that buying decorations in the 1930s would save you even more?

3. Better yet, instead of store-bought decorations, decorate with nature! Bring the outside in with the fresh scent of cut evergreen limbs and live chipmunks. While these lovable critters will delight your children, be warned that they're fond of cuddling in warm places, so always check before turning on that toaster oven!

4. And don't throw out your cottage cheese containers, as these will make great gift boxes for the Christmas ornaments that you are going to assemble from old key chains and discarded condom wrappers.

5. And for Christmas dinner, who needs an expensive Butterball when every town has an animal shelter chockfull of meaty strays?
6. Don't have enough money for a new Christmas sweater? A few Popsicle sticks and some Elmer's glue can turn any tattered sweatshirt into a glorious Nativity scene! Give your wise men candy-cane staffs to give a real Christmas feel to this classic Bible setting. And did you know that pubic hair makes excellent manger hay?
7. Did you miss this season's big sales? No worries, as you can beat those rock-bottom Black Friday prices by taking up the profitable hobby of shoplifting. Studies show that only one out of four shoplifters is ever caught and fewer still are prosecuted. And if you are incarcerated, you're eligible to receive the services of a public defender *free of charge.* Now, that's a steal!
8. Instead of the usual exchange of meaningless gift cards for store merchandise, how about creating your own gift certificates for personalized services? Whether it's making waffles or cleaning the parakeet cage, be sure that you can perform the task well and that the gift is appropriate for the recipient. No matter how skilled you may be, let your in-laws find their own massage therapist.

ENTERPRISE

TO MAKE MONEY, YOU MUST TAKE MONEY.

First Class (As I Imagine)

My Auto Mechanic: Is that the new Yacht Buyer's Guide?

My Son's Orthodontist: I'm finished with it. You can take it if you like.

My Auto Mechanic: Are you sure? It looked like you might still be reading.

My Son's Orthodontist: No, I'm done. Besides, I already have a luxury yacht.

My Auto Mechanic: Oh, thanks. I'm looking for a second one myself.

My Son's Orthodontist: Oh?

My Auto Mechanic: For my Mediterranean home.

My Son's Orthodontist: Of course. One word of advice: I wouldn't get anything less than a 60-footer.

My Auto Mechanic: Oh, definitely. I'll need the space for the walk-in humidor.

My Son's Orthodontist: Good thinking. You got to have a walk-in humidor.

FLIGHT ATTENDANT: Sir, would you like another glass of Dom Perignon?

MY SON'S ORTHODONTIST: That would be great, thank you. And while you're at it, could you grab me a pair of those mink slippers? My feet are getting a little chilly.

FLIGHT ATTENDANT: Right away, sir. And for you?

MY AUTO MECHANIC: I'll just have more of the lobster soaked in caviar.

FLIGHT ATTENDANT: My pleasure, sir.

MY SON'S ORTHODONTIST: So, are you going to Paris on business?

MY AUTO MECHANIC: No, my wife needs me to pick up a coffee table she bought, a Louie something or other.

MY SON'S ORTHODONTIST: The honey-dos never end, do they?

MY AUTO MECHANIC: You got that right! So what do you do?

MY SON'S ORTHODONTIST: When I'm not sailing, I'm usually golfing. Every now and then I'll fix an overbite, though, to pay the bills.

MY AUTO MECHANIC: Ah, tooth business? Nice!

MY SON'S ORTHODONTIST: How about yourself?

MY AUTO MECHANIC: I guess you could say I'm in the cosmetic-surgery business myself.

MY SON'S ORTHODONTIST: Oh?

My Auto Mechanic: I own and operate an auto-repair shop.

My Son's Orthodontist: I have to ask—do you ever charge for an unnecessary repair?

My Auto Mechanic: I would never take advantage of an unsuspecting customer.

(Bursts into laughter)

My Son's Orthodontist: (laughing, too) For a second, I thought you were serious.

My Auto Mechanic: Yeah, I had a guy last week who had a burnt-out brake light. I convinced him that he had a short in his fuse-monitoring system—whatever that is. Eight hundred dollars!

My Son's Orthodontist: And this trip is being paid for by the removal of a perfectly healthy tooth.

My Auto Mechanic: Sweet!

My Son's Orthodontist: No, sweet tooth!

(They both laugh. As they wipe tears from their eyes, a woman returning to her seat approaches them.)

My Wife's Therapist: Excuse me. Is that the new Yacht Buyer's Guide?

Dan McQuinn

An Open Letter to the Employees of Chromatic Enterprises

Dear Chromatic Employees:

By now you have surely seen the press reports alleging misappropriation of corporate funds and questioning the governance of Chromatic Enterprises. While our company policy is to not comment on rumors and gossip, I feel compelled under the circumstances to set the record straight so Chromatic Enterprises can continue to provide superior souvenir lighters to tobacco lovers worldwide without interruption.

Before I address the allegations, I would like to say that it is with great pride that I serve as your president and chief operating officer, and I continue to be amazed by the successes achieved by Chromatic employees. From the battery of attorneys vigorously defending us against any one of the thousands of liability suits brought against Chromatic each year to the tireless assembly workers toiling for one of our Third World affiliates, Chromatic employees never lose sight of what matters most: our customers. For it's our customers who look to us not just for a light but for a product that makes them feel good about themselves, especially when they smoke. As long as Chromatic employees stay focused on these customers, I know we will see ourselves through this current crisis.

As you may know, the recent disclosure of low-interest, off-balance sheet loans by Chromatic to my brother has gained much attention from the headline-hungry media. The fact that these loans were used to build a private ski lodge has also raised some eyebrows. I can assure you that not only were the recording of these loans well within the bounds of generally accepted accounting principles, but these financing activities were viewed as sound investments that would benefit Chromatic shareholders. If completed, the Timber Wolf Lodge would have served as a premier executive conference center and a first-class facility for holding shareholder meetings. Unfortunately, construction of the project was halted when a court ruled that the resort was being built on lands protected to *preserve* timber wolves. Needless to say, you won't be seeing Robert Redford attending a Chromatic board meeting any time soon.

Because of the economic hardships brought on by the "timber wolf chapter" in our corporate history and the general downturn in the tobacco-accessory industry due to reduced teen smoking, Chromatic is being forced to make drastic cuts in expenditures. A company never likes to tell its employees that there is not enough work, but tomorrow morning we will be sending an e-mail with that message to 12,000 of you. As we say goodbye to our many colleagues, let me assure you that these decisions do not come easy, and pain is being felt in the executive suite as well. The elimination of gourmet dining services in the corporate jet fleet will be especially burdensome.

The media feeding frenzy has also brought attention to my personal life. My family and I have endured a barrage of tabloid scrutiny after last Tuesday's discovery of a dead prostitute's body in the tool shed of my new Lake Forest home. While I would like to speak freely to share with the public the "facts" to clear my name, counsel has advised me not to comment on the specifics of this case, as authorities are still conducting their investigation. For now, let me just say that for the next house I purchase, I will not skimp on the home inspection.

With all the attention given to these unfortunate developments, a small minority of shareholders are demanding my resignation. These professional lobbyists equate bad luck with mismanagement and if given the chance would have impeached Abraham Lincoln during the Civil War. I for one will not stand for this kind of vigilante justice running amok. While a resignation would certainly save me some further personal embarrassment, I feel too strongly

about the shareholders and employees
of Chromatic to consider such a move.
Chromatic needs the experience I have
gained during these troublesome times to
lead it back to its former glory.

   For those of you who have written or
e-mailed to voice your support, I thank
you. Why just yesterday I received an
inspirational note from a young worker
in our soon-to-be-closed Kentucky plant.
It had only four simple words: *May you
burn eternally*. Obviously referring to
our flagship, long-lasting Elite lighter
series, this metaphor could not better
sum up my feelings about Chromatic and
its employees. *May we all burn eternally
together!*

   Faithfully yours,
   Richard Face
   President and CEO
   Chromatic Enterprises

Dan McQuinn

OUR PRIVACY POLICY

PROTECTING YOUR PRIVACY is job one at State Penn Mutual. Policyholders like you have trusted us with their insurance needs for over 20 years, and we take our obligation to safeguard your personal information seriously, as we are a very serious company. This document is intended to give you a better understanding of how the information we gather about you is used and protected.

THE INFORMATION WE COLLECT

- We obtain information about you from you directly, from your transactions with us and third parties including your employer, physician and state motor vehicle departments.[1]
- Any party who performs services for us is required to safeguard customer information and may use it only in connection with performing such services.[2]
- We will not sell your information to third parties.[3]

---

1. And your ex-wife, who really opens up after a few apricot stone sours.
2. Unless they have a very good reason otherwise.
3. Fourth, fifth and sixth parties are fair game.

- We secure and limit access to your information to the extent that if you contact our customer-service representatives, they will claim not to know you and deny your very existence.

At any time, we may access from identity thieves the following information about you:

- Name (first, middle, last, secret porn)
- Address
- Phone number
- Social Security number
- SAT scores
- STD history
- The amount of weed you consumed in college
- Your reasons for never completing college[4]
- The true story of why you were sent home early from summer camp

THE INFORMATION WE DISCLOSE

Information about our customers will be disclosed only as required by law.[5] We may share information with organizations that need the information to perform a professional function, including:

---

4. See weed question above.
5. Unless we discover something really juicy.

- Other insurance companies
- Employers
- Government and law-enforcement agencies
- Jehovah's Witnesses
- Dr. Phil
- *The National Enquirer*
- The Ku Klux Klan

In the event that the information we share is of an embarrassing or personal nature,[6] we will always provide it with the utmost decorum and appropriate disclaimers. For example, whenever we release information about your inordinate number of claims for erectile-dysfunction medication, we will always include a statement to the effect that "it is common problem affecting most men."

CONFIDENTIALITY AND SECURITY

Our employees are trained to safeguard your information, as we've learned that secure information brings more value on the open market. We are thus careful to hire only employees who are good at keeping secrets.[7] We also use the latest in physical and procedural data-storage methods, having obtained exclusive rights to the mayonnaise jars on Funk & Wagnalls' porch.

---

6. And it usually is.
7. Our staff consists primarily of adulterers, she-males and members of organized crime.

On-Line Security

As part of our continuous improvement efforts, we track how visitors use our Web site and regularly gather data on how our customers navigate the World Wide Web. We are particularly interested in identifying the Web sites that provide users with the most intensive online experience. For example, we regularly track "money sites," which are the last sites visited by a customer in a given pornographic Web session. This information is shared internally with a select group of individuals who can best be described as "guys in the office who like this sort of thing." Rest assured that discretion is paramount, as all steps possible are taken to ensure that nobody's wife ever finds out. Links to sites involving bestiality or other unusual acts of perversion are also archived and e-mailed anonymously to the girl in accounting with the big rack.

Special Notice for Tennessee Residents

The provisions of this policy are not in effect for residents of the state of Tennessee. As everyone in this state is already related, the issue of privacy is moot.

What to Do if I Have a Privacy Concern

If you have a concern about privacy or security, by all means do not tell anyone, including us, as this is the only way that we can ensure that further breeches in privacy do not occur. At all cost, do not talk to anyone, even family and clergy.[8] If you must tell someone, spill your guts to your bartender. He doesn't care about your life and will only remember the size of your tip.

This privacy policy may be changed at any time at our whim. We will mail you a new policy in the event that we make significant changes.[9] You will never read this document and, when disposing of it, will most likely be too lazy to separate for recycling. In fact, you are probably not even reading this document now. So if I were to call you a big, fat asswipe, we probably would not even receive one complaint.[10]

---

8. Clergy especially will hold confessions over your head, extracting favors that will invariably turn into more secrets.
9. Or if we need to camouflage a rate increase.
10. And you definitely are not reading the footnotes. Asswipe! Asswipe! Asswipe!

Attitudes

Mr. Kenneth Owens
Louisville, Kentucky
March 30, 2009

Hugo Thomas International, Inc.
850 Madison Avenue
New York, New York 10022

To Whom It May Concern:

As a longtime customer of your fashionable undergarments, it is with great disappointment that I seek a refund for a recent purchase of a personal-care product. Simply put, the *Attitudes by Hugo Thomas* Deodorant Stick did not live up to its advertised benefits.

Not only did the *Attitudes* fragrance neglect to provide "a cool, crisp freshness complementing the many dimensions of the modern man," but it also failed to attract vivacious cover girls yearning to "bask in the sensual warmth of sheer, exotic woods." Quite the contrary, when wearing *Attitudes*, I would repel even the most desperate barroom skank. And no wonder—instead of emitting the "light and fruity aroma of intoxicating spices," your deodorant smothered me in an odor that can best be described as that of "rotting cantaloupes."

According to my legal counsel, your negligence has subjected me to severe mental anguish, and if I were to put my case before a jury, collecting substantial punitive damages would be "a cakewalk." I, though, seek only to be reimbursed for my initial purchase amount and the postage associated with this correspondence. Enclosed you will find the partially used deodorant stick in question, along with my original receipt. Payment by cash, check or money order will suffice.

Sincerely,

Kenneth Owens

Trent Simpson
Customer Relations
Hugo Thomas Intl.
April 21, 2009

Mr. Kenneth Owens
Louisville, KY

Dear Mr. Owens,

In my 12 years of customer-relations experience, I have come across a wide gamut of scoundrels intent on defrauding the honest businesses that form the bedrock of this nation. But in all my years of dealing with such con artists, I have never come across a letter as brash and self-serving as the one sent by you to our offices last month.

Attitudes by Hugo Thomas is a premier men's fragrance that is used daily by millions of men worldwide without incident. While our advertising does portray our clientele as successful trendsetters who attract a following among both sexes, we in no way promise or guarantee that use of our product will allow you to achieve the same.

To hold Hugo Thomas responsible for your failure to attract a one-night-stand partner is disturbingly pathetic. While a good deodorant can certainly enhance a romantic encounter, it is only one factor in the natural selection of

the species and is no substitute for
favorable genetics or natural charisma.
Before blaming your antiperspirant, take
a long, hard look at yourself. Have you
been to a gym recently? Do you engage
in interesting conversation? And in
what decade was your current wardrobe
obtained?

As for your claims of product
nonperformance, we here at Hugo
Thomas are wondering if the product
is being used as directed. *Attitudes*
works best when it is applied to the
underarm area and the underarm area
only. Rubbing *Attitudes* on clothing,
other appendages or orifices can result
in unintended olfactory interactions.
Nor should *Attitudes* be used with
other products. Dime store colognes,
acne creams and arousal-enhancement
ointments only lessen the effectiveness
of the fragrance. The experience of
our customers is that *Attitudes* is most
effective when coupled with good health
and grooming habits. Diet, hygiene
and tobacco use can all contribute to
unwanted aromas and should be reviewed
before making wild accusations against
one's deodorant supplier.

As far as the alleged cantaloupe
stench, our experts are baffled. However,
it is not uncommon in cases like this to
discover later that the person reporting
the problem has been participating in
some type of deviant sexual practice,
usually involving a household pet.

Even if we could believe your implausible claim, we would be unable to provide you a refund, because of our inability to validate your proof of purchase. The deodorant stick that you returned is clearly labeled "SAMPLE – NOT TO BE SOLD OR RESOLD," and the receipt you provided appears to have originated from a pet store (no surprise here) with the words *Hugo Thomas Attitudes $65.00* scrawled in pencil. Given that Hugo Thomas has authorized only the finest boutiques to sell its brands and caters only to humans, the validity of your purchase claim is questionable at best.

As far as your veiled threats of litigation, my only response is, "We have attorneys too!" Based upon the legal advice you've been given, though, I hope for your sake that what you are paying for counsel is not any more than what you apparently have paid for our deodorant.

In short, we are returning your original deodorant stick and rejecting your refund request for the reasons stated above.

Sincerely,

Trent Simpson
Hugo Thomas International

Dan McQuinn

Mr. Kenneth Owens
Louisville, Kentucky
May 1, 2009

Hugo Thomas International
850 Madison Avenue
New York, New York 10022

Mr. Simpson:

While you did not elaborate on your "12 years of customer relations experience," I can only assume by the tone of your response that you held positions somewhere in the bowels of our nation's system of penitentiaries. Where else could someone learn to mistrust the clientele that otherwise pays for his three-martini lunches and country-club memberships?

However, when I more closely examine the perverse logic you espouse, I begin to think the large bright sign above your conscience has been flashing "vacant" for some time. Did your mother use narcotics during her pregnancy? Were you ignored as an infant? Why else would someone characterize a company that charges $65 for a 2-ounce bottle of scented tap water as an honest enterprise that is vital to our national interests?

If you spent less time berating your customers and more time tending to the details of your business operations, you would realize that your precious brand is being peddled in every pet store and gas-station mini-mart north of the equator. The fact that your product is regularly mislabeled is just another example of your company's inattention to detail and disregard for your customers. To hold these unfortunate patrons liable for your own bungling is inexcusable and reprehensible.

I stand behind my original request. If met with further resistance, I can guarantee that the next letter you receive will be from my attorney (who lives quite handsomely on the proceeds from consumer-fraud lawsuits, I might add).

Sincerely,

Kenneth Owens

Dan McQuinn

> Trent Simpson
> Customer Relations
> Hugo Thomas, Inc.
> June 10, 2009

Mr. Kenneth Owens
Louisville, KY

Mr. Owens,

I must point out that the deodorant stick that you continue to include with your unintelligible manifestos appears to have been consumed further since your last correspondence. Since none of our mail carriers reek of intoxicating spices (or rotting fruit), I can only assume that you continue to use this product in spite of your claims of dissatisfaction.

The only logical explanation for your increasingly irrational behavior is that you have totally lost your grip on reality. As such, we have decided to take drastic steps to remedy this situation. Beginning next week, you should receive the first in a series of complimentary shipments of Obsession by Calvin Klein—our principal competitor in the field of sophisticated scents for men.

Why are we taking this action? Do we feel responsible for your predicament? Are we intimidated by your threats of legal action? Hardly. Your country-lawyer tactics aside, the real reason for making such a grand gesture is not coming from our legal department but our marketing group. Simply put, they have determined that keeping you as a customer is a greater liability than your business is worth. Congratulations, Mr. Owens! You have graduated from being a mild nuisance to the worst customer a company can have—the customer who you are embarrassed is using your product.

One day if we decide to go after the Jerry Springer demographic, we may want you back. Until then, however, enjoy the "refreshing, oriental, woody fragrance" of Obsession and forward any further complaints and/or extortion letters to:

> Calvin Klein, Inc.
> 200 W. 39th St.
> New York, NY 10018

Our corporate security has insisted that we cut off further communications with you and as a precautionary measure has retained your deodorant stick as evidence. Your letters are also being kept on file: Under "N" for *Nut-Job*!

Sincerely,

Trent Simpson
Hugo Thomas, International

Dan McQuinn

Found in My Pocket

I have personally examined every detail of this garment to make sure it meets our high quality standards. In this time of global uncertainty, you can take solace in knowing that your apparel has been thoroughly scrutinized to assure your complete satisfaction.

Your comfort and gratification is a personal quest. While other inspectors simply examine a piece of fabric for visual indications of flawed workmanship, I pride myself on taking a completely holistic approach to quality assurance. In addition to the routine "look and pull" methods performed by my colleagues, I employ a battery of tests to ensure your garment's utility, including assessments for stain resistance, wrinkle avoidance, washability, flammability, durability, tactile appeal, odor absorption and taste.

After such a regimen, most inspectors would collapse like a Greek bank. I, however, am just gathering steam and immerse myself in your attire, checking its form, fit and aesthetic appeal. Still not content, I subject your apparel to a series of everyday simulations. You'll be pleased to know that your

Kids Say the Cutest Things When They're Drunk

slacks performed particularly well during the square dancing exercise, both with and without undergarments.

Emboldened by success, I took your pants out of the laboratory and to "the streets," where their performance could be observed under real-world conditions. So while other inspectors were pretending to be working late while making love to one of their many mistresses, I continued to put your clothing through its paces. I'm pleased to report that your garment performed flawlessly while executing such tasks as boarding a bus, bending to look for a dropped transfer token and walking six miles for not being able to produce said token to one overly surly driver.

Fortunately, the unplanned hike provided me additional "pants time" and the opportunity to view your apparel's response to further stimuli. An impromptu visit to a filling-station restroom allowed me to observe the ease with which the stainless steel zipper glides up and down its contoured path. I also witnessed how quickly the Space Age fabric absorbs foreign contaminants when faced with excessive dribbling conditions. With just one single-ply sheet of low-grade bathroom paper, I was able to completely dry unsightly stains, with only slight traces of tissue residue remaining. Now, that's performance when it counts!

Rejuvenated, I continued my trek with your slacks, which retained their crisp look and addictive comfort every step of the way. After almost a full day of flawless execution, I came upon my favorite cinema and decided it was time to reward your pants with a night of leisure. As I received my change from the attendant, I could not help but notice her "checking out" how your classic-fit khakis accentuated my buttocks—a historic problem area for me. I made a mental note to suggest a new warning a label for this garment: "Caution—Provocative Stares May Be Triggered by Wearing these Lady-Killers."

Unfazed, I entered the viewing booth, where the show was exhilarating, to say the least. In fact, the performance was so exciting that I finished early with extra quarters to spare. Unfortunately, your trousers did not survive unscathed. I'm sure if you wash in warm water and tumble-dry per the care instructions found on the inner waistband, your pants will be returned to their pristine condition. I am, though, too tired to test this hypothesis. Rather, I am going to spend the remainder of the evening putting your pants through one last set of obstacles as I try to locate an all-night doughnut shop.

I only hope that when these pants finally leave my legs and adorn yours, you appreciate my humble work and are able to receive the same level of enjoyment from your purchase as I did. Thank you for buying our product.

Inspector #9

Circular Jerk

— Hello, this is Claire, your Circular Wireless virtual customer-service agent. How may I help you today?

— This is Doug. Uhh, I'd like to report a lost phone ...

— "Lost phone" is not a recognizable option.

— What the?

— "What the" is not a recognizable option.

For instructions in Spanish, press or say *uno*.
For instructions in French, press or say *deux*.
For instructions in Pig Latin, press or say *eethray*.
And for instructions in English, scream any obscenity.

— Shit!

— You selected *shit*.

For questions pertaining to any of the following, please state the name of the option. You may choose from questions regarding:

Dan McQuinn

  shitty service,
  billing errors,
  spotty coverage,
  exorbitant roaming fees
  and the unreadable terms of your service contract.

— Shitty service!

— You selected "shitty service."

Please press or say your Circular Wireless phone number so that we may obtain your account information from our database.

— 555-476-8195.

— Hold on, please, while we obtain your information.

 (Music on hold)

I'm sorry, you entered an invalid number. Please press or say your Circular Wireless phone number again.

— 555-476-8195.

— Hold on, please, while we obtain your information.

 (Music on hold)

I'm sorry, you entered an invalid number again. You must really be stupid. If you would like to speak with a live representative, please say *live representative.*

— Live representative!

— Please hold while I connect you to a Circular Wireless customer-service representative.

(Music on hold)

I'm sorry. All of our representatives are currently taking cigarette breaks. Please stay on the line for the next available agent.

Are you tired of wasting time? With the Circular Wireless EZ payment program, Circular Wireless can withdraw payments from your savings account at any time, relieving you of the hassle of reviewing complex bills and billing plans. To let Circular Wireless do all the work of depleting your savings, just say *EZ payment plan* to your Circular Wireless customer-service representative.

(Music on hold)

— Hello, this is Tyrone. How may I direct your call?

— Oh, I lost my cell phone, and I need to get a new one.

— What's your phone number?

— Didn't Claire tell you?

— Who?

— Never mind. The number is 555-476-8195.

Dan McQuinn

— Hold on, please.

— No, wait!

— Are you tired of wasting money? Let Circular Wireless help you save with our Circular Wireless Pyramid Plus plan. For only $99.99 a month, you can get up to 12,000 minutes of calling per month for life during non-peak calling times. To start saving money today, just say *Pyramid Plus* to your Circular Wireless customer-service representative.

Non-peak hours are considered midnight to 3 A.M. Monday through Wednesday. All other calls are at $1.85 per minute. Lifetime service contracts subject to availability based upon local indentured-servitude laws.

(Music on hold)

— Hello, this is Tyrone. How may I direct your call?

— I talked to you 20 minutes ago. I lost my phone and wanted info on how to get a new one.

— What is your phone number?

— 555-476-8195!

— Sir, you have a business calling plan. I can only handle consumer accounts.

— It's my own phone. I just bought through my employer because my company gets a discount.

— You're going to have to call our business customer-service number. That number is 888-560-4188.

— But I called the phone number listed on my statement!

— Sorry, sir. I can't help you. Would you like me to connect you to our business customer-service line?

— Please!

— Are you in a rut? Are you tired of not getting anywhere? If you like working with machines and can pass a drug test given three tries, a career at Circular Wireless may be for you. To start your new life today, just say *new life* when you speak with your Circular Wireless customer-service representative.

(Music on hold)

— Hello, this is Carl. How may I direct your call?

— Yes! I lost my cell phone. My phone number is 555-476-8195. I would like to shut off service on the old phone and get a new one. Do not put me on hold!

— One moment, please.

— No! I've been on hold—oh my God—all night. Better yet, I'd like to talk to a manager.

— But I am fully capable of helping you.

— I'm sure you are, but at this point I would rather speak to a manager.

— Sure, I'll connect you.

(Music on hold)

— Are you tired of hearing worrisome rumors about cranial tumor growth related to cell-phone usage? Are you tired of being made to feel like a fool by misinformed scare tactics? With Circular Wireless's "Debunking the Tumor Myth: Fighting Ignorance with Ignorance" pamphlet, Circular Wireless has manufactured a set of cell-phone safety statistics that will put even the most persistent know-it-all egghead on the defensive. Just say *tumor factoids* the next time you speak with your Circular Wireless customer-service representative.

— Hello, this is Clarisse, your Circular Wireless virtual customer-service manager. How may I help you?

— Another machine! Fuck you, Clarisse!

— "Fuck you" is an option.

(Dial tone)

Order

Rule-makers make the best rule-breakers.

Encyclopedia Brown Today: Solutions from the NYPD Case File

The Case of the Midtown Pickax Killer

Benjamin Reilly said he never heard of Dr. Haggerty, but he knew too much about him. He knew that Dr. Haggerty was (1) a man, not a woman, and (2) a dentist, not a doctor. How else could he explain his off-color joke that he would make at victim No. 4's expense: "Did you check to see if *he* had any new *cavities*?"

Suspicions were confirmed later when Benjamin, left alone in the interrogation room, stacked a set of dominoes in the same crisscross pattern as the bodies found in the back of the ice cream truck. Of course, the dominoes had deliberately been left behind by Encyclopedia, a trick he had learned from his father in *The Case of the Missing Yo-Yo*.

When tripped up by his fibs, Benjamin confessed to the murders, and *The Case of the Midtown Pickax Killer* was closed.

Dan McQuinn

The Case of the Missing Heroin

Encyclopedia won his bet with Sally Kimball. Both the leader of the Vice Lords and the cabdriver spoke the truth. The briefcase carrying the heroin was blue but appeared to be gray because the cabdriver was *colorblind*.

Once Encyclopedia determined that the cabdriver was telling the truth, it was easy to find the contraband heroin. The cabdriver, unable to distinguish the color of his cargo, mistakenly gave the gang leader's briefcase to the businessman exiting the taxi. From the cabdriver's testimony that the passenger had mud on his shoes, Encyclopedia was able to surmise that the businessman had attended the groundbreaking at the civic center earlier in the afternoon. Thanks to guest lists from the ceremony, the briefcase and heroin were quickly found and retrieved from a very surprised executive.

The gang leader was arrested for trafficking narcotics and is awaiting trial, while the cabdriver was freed from the precinct lockup surviving a brutal rape attempt. Sally Kimball made good on her promise, and Encyclopedia was rewarded with the best-tasting piece of blueberry pie in all of New York City!

Kids Say the Cutest Things When They're Drunk

THE CASE OF THE EMBARRASSED POLITICIAN

When the mayor plunked two dimes and nickel on the gas can on Detective Brown's desk, Encyclopedia had no idea that his next investigation would result in the arrest of a prominent government official.

Councilman Paxson claimed he had not had inappropriate relations with the woman who entered his hotel room. He also insisted he did not know she was 17 or a prostitute. This testimony directly contradicted that of the bellhop who said Paxson approached him earlier asking, "Where can I find a teenage prostitute?"

With no physical evidence, how would Encyclopedia determine who was telling the truth? Encyclopedia recalled a similar incident in the case of the missing pickle jar where he tricked Bugs Meany into confessing that he stole the jar by falsely accusing him of stealing a watermelon as well. By telling Councilman Paxson that the prostitute claimed she was now pregnant with his love child, Encyclopedia forced the political leader to refute the accusation and acknowledge that the prostitute was in fact male, proving the councilman had carnal knowledge of his visitor.

In the end, just as the councilman had done, Encyclopedia got his man. And Encyclopedia delivered the news of the breakthrough personally to the mayor, returning the 25 cents to the city.

Dan McQuinn

Henchman Wanted

Wanted: Hardened criminal to assist evil genius in committing notorious felonies accompanied by outlandish pranks. Applicants should be tough, menacing and display dimwitted allegiance to misguided authority. Prison record a plus. Serious inquiries only.

```
                         Evil Nemesis Enterprises
                      Department of Human Resources
                                   Gotham City, USA
                                      April 1, 2011

Mr. Ivan Lackey
1000 Broken Arrow Way
Apt. 3B
Gotham City, USA

Dear Mr. Lackey,

    On behalf of Evil Nemesis Enterprises
Inc., we are pleased to offer you the
position of senior henchman, reporting
directly to your supervisor, the Joker,
who as the Clown Prince of Crime is
responsible for all felonious activities
```

in the greater Gotham metro area. Your anticipated start date will be Monday, April 1.

Your annual base salary will be $45,000, payable biweekly. As a senior henchman, you will also be eligible to participate in the Evil Felon Bonus Plan, which will entitle you to up to 10 percent of the net receipts of any job you participate in, "the take," subject to withholding for taxes, insurance and Evil Nemesis Christmas Club deductions. Your actual percentage of receipts will be mutually agreed upon between you and your manager, subject to revisions due to chicanery.

Company regulations require that all henchpersons wear a uniform. Color-coded masks and shirts are provided by the company, and you will be responsible for wearing the correct colors for each day you work per a schedule published by your supervisor. The company will also provide large gunnysacks for hauling loot and use as a weapon when filled. Pants and shoes are to be provided by the employee and should be dress-black (no gym shoes!). All clothing shall be clean and neatly pressed for each workday. You are responsible for all dry-cleaning costs, although such costs may be tax-deductible. Please contact an accountant or professional tax adviser for specific tax questions.

You will be eligible for coverage under the Evil Nemesis Benefits Plan on the first day of the month following completion of ninety (90) days of employment. Your benefits include a medical plan that covers all on-the-job injuries, including those sustained while fighting law-enforcement officials and vigilante crusaders. Such injuries should be minimal, though, as your organization prides itself on always outnumbering your opponent. Furthermore, our experience has been that our staff quickly recovers from even the most violent blows to the head. You will also being working in an environment with high noise levels (e.g. *pow*, *kaboom*, *zowie*) and are encouraged to wear ear protection. The company will provide reusable earplugs that, in addition to protecting your hearing, will allow you to bungle mind-numbingly simple orders from your evil master.

Under standard vacation policy, you will be eligible for one week of vacation pay after six (6) months of continuous employment. Two weeks' vacation is granted after one (1) year of employment. Please note that incarceration time does not count as service time in the calculation of vacation benefits. However, you may be eligible for "flex time off" at the discretion of your manager and with the approval/consent of the Human Resources Department.

Our offer is contingent upon your completing our pre-employment reference verification, application process and medical examination, which includes a drug screen to ensure usage of illegal drugs prior to your first day of employment.

This offer of employment is open for a period of five (5) days from the date of this letter. Within this time frame, I would appreciate your confirming your acceptance by signing below and returning this letter to me.

On your start date, report to the third floor of the abandoned toy warehouse on the outskirts of Gotham City. Signs pointing to the Evil Lair should be clearly marked. On your first day, please bring copies of your birth certificate and criminal rap sheet.

We do believe you have the qualities for success at Evil Nemesis Enterprises Inc., and we feel confident that you will find crime with us both challenging and rewarding. Please call if you have any questions or if I can be of any assistance to you.

Sincerely,

Robert Powell
Director, Human Resources
Evil Nemesis Enterprises

I hereby accept this offer of employment.

Ivan Lackey   Date

Dan McQuinn

Great Moments in the American Revolution (If I Were There)

The Crossing of the Delaware

Are you sure we want to cross here? The river is full of sharp rocks, and that boat doesn't look very seaworthy. Besides, who wants to take an open-air boat ride in the middle of winter?

I'm not doubting you. No, you don't have to repeat the apple-tree story again. I get it. You're very trustworthy. I'm just saying, wouldn't we better off if we found a sturdy bridge? I could swear there's one not far from here, a few miles at most. Better yet, if we could find a nice inn with a warm fire that serves mulled cider ... I just think we'd fare better if we were well rested. Come to think of it, I'm almost sure I saw an inn near the bridge.

No, we're not running away. It's a tactical move. If we wait a month or two at the warm inn while the British are stuck outside in the cold air, we could freeze them out! Their resistance will be run down and we won't even need to attack. As soon as those Redcoats see us crossing the bridge carrying warm blankets and cider, they'll be lining up to surrender!

Did I mention that the inn has a Ladies Night?

THE DECLARATION OF INDEPENDENCE

Yes, I've started a first draft. So far so good. Still working on the middle and end, but the beginning is strong.

How does it go?

I don't like to tip my hand too early. You know, it might sound funny out of context. Besides, I'm a firm believer that too many cooks can spoil the broth.

I understand you're not "a cook." It was just a figure of speech.

I know that you're paying for the manuscript.

Of course, I know which end of the quill is sharp.

Hey! There's no reason to get violent!

OK, if you insist, then here it goes, "We the white male landowners, in order to form a more perfect club ..." — That's all I have right now.

Too limiting?

I suppose I could simplify it. With all due respect, though, it sounds a little bland just saying "we the people," but you know best.

Sure, I have other ideas. I like browsing *Poor Richard's Almanac* for inspiration, but I tend to lose myself in it. It's so addictive! It's like having all of the world's knowledge right at your fingertips—and it's so easy to get distracted by the salty parts!

So I was thinking about doing the rest of the piece from the perspective of a freed slave, you know, an ironic take.

You don't like irony?

And you think it could give *them* ideas.

OK, we can forget the race angle and just stick to a straight declaration. It's going to be cutting it close, though, as the 24th is only a few weeks away.

What do you mean the 4th? I could swear you said the 24th. Are you sure?

One last question: We're on the King's side, right?

THE BOSTON TEA PARTY

Why is everyone dressed as Indians? When you said we'd all be wearing costumes, nobody said anything to me about a theme.

Very funny. No, I'm not a prostitute. If you must know, I'm supposed to be one of those butter-churner ladies. And no, I didn't sew the undergarments myself—I got them from your mother. Zing!

So there's only tea on board? No gunpowder? Ammunition? Rum?

Kids Say the Cutest Things When They're Drunk

And I can't believe we're just dumping it all in the harbor. This is the good East India stuff. I usually can only afford Colonial. If I only knew, I would have brought the wagon and filled up.

Those are big crates. You know, my doctor says I should avoid heavy lifting. Darn back spasms—always seem to flare up when there's work to be done!

Maybe I can just be a lookout instead? I can wait on shore. I'll start a fire and if I see anybody coming, I'll send up some smoke signals. Get it?

I can also have some tea brewing for you as well. Did anyone bring a kettle?

Never mind, I should be able to find one in town. I'll have to take the getaway carriage, though.

Of course I'll be back. How far can I get dressed as a butter churner?

Trust me.

Dan McQuinn

Instructions for Voting

District 13 Voter:

This ballot has been carefully designed by the Madison County Board of Elections to provide the most user-friendly interface possible for participating in the democratic process, given current fiscal restraints.

Because of archaic state law (thank you, Progressive Reform Movement!), all eligible candidates must be listed on the ballot, even wacko parties who don't have a snowball's prayer in hell. Yes, we're talking about you, Sons of the Klan!

The order in which nominees are listed on the ballot is based on a random drawing, with names picked from a hat once worn by John Wilkes Booth. *The Hat*, a fixture in Madison County elections for nearly a century, provides an air of historical significance to an otherwise-mundane chore and is featured prominently in the county's *Assassins Remembered* traveling school exhibit.

For each selection, darken the oval using the supplied No. 2 pencil. Do not circle the oval, mark with an "X" or insert a check mark. And definitely do not try to convert the oval to an emoticon. Please do not identify yourself. If your ballot is signed, your name will be included on the county Web site for known sex offenders and your vote will be discarded in a pagan ceremony involving fire and virgin blood.

Please fill out only one ballot per voter, as this is not *American Idol*. Please also leave your pencil for the next voter, as we are not the Welcome Wagon either.

Voting is restricted to U.S. citizens, 18 years and older, who are registered to vote at least 20 days prior to Election Day. If you're registering to buy a gun, though, you only have to wait three days. And if you do bring a gun into the voting booth, please make sure it is unloaded or at least the safety is on.

Prior to voting, all felony convictions must be completed. Also, citizens may not have been found as legally incompetent by a state court within the past year. So before you vote, it's important to consider the timing of any planned criminal activity and subsequent insanity pleas. As we like to say down at the Board of Elections, before you pull the trigger, remember when you need to pull the lever. Although in this county we don't actually vote with levers—see aforementioned No. 2 pencils.

As the election judges are volunteers and typically older than the internal-combustion engine, please be patient. Someday you may outlive those who share common interests and find that monitoring an election is your only escape from endless days of watching the Game Show Network at peak volume. So if you find yourself stuck talking to an election judge about back pain or sugar rationing, just nod—and return your pencil.

Please select only candidates who are listed on the ballot. If you think you're the first person clever enough to submit Mr. Potato Head as a write-in candidate, you're not. In fact, if such votes were allowed, Mr. Potato Head would have been our 43rd president. Some would argue this happened anyway.

There are many judges and committeemen on today's ballot, so please do not dawdle. Everyone knows that these positions do not matter. Just pick the one with the name whose ethnicity most closely matches your own and be done with it.

In case you're wondering why we're still using paper ballots in the 21st century, you probably don't remember last year's proposition to increase funding for the Board of Elections. And you undoubtedly don't remember that a portion of this increase would have funded a study exploring options for automating the voting process—as well as providing long-overdue raises for election officials! And you definitely don't remember that 97% of you voted against this measure.

So if you would now like to cast a vote for this proposal, you can find the proposition on page—oh, that's right, there is no proposition on this ballot thanks to lack of support for this summer's petition drive! We know you were home. We saw the lights on. So if you wrist hurts from filling in ovals, you can sharpen your No. 2 pencil and stick it in the orifice of your choice. After all, this is an election.

Thank you for voting today.

The Madison County Board of Elections

Dan McQuinn

Vote for Bob

Bob Gorman knows that life is futile. He knows that no matter what we do, we are all going to die. And if elected to Congress, Bob pledges that his vision of futility will come to fruition.

Bob will not waste effort on needless legislation or senseless initiatives. While other candidates promise reform, Bob knows that meaningful change is impossible, as all laws are pointless. He knows that no regulation can change our fate, as we are all destined to an eternity of irrelevance.

Bob will not raise your taxes, as he understands that material possessions are fleeting. He knows that all matter is of equal insignificance whether it be gold bullion or the dust of our grandchildren's corpses.

Bob will not support efforts to save the environment, as he knows that one day the sun will extinguish itself and the Earth will become a dark, frigid hulk devoid of all life. Bob does not worry about global warming because he knows that our carbon footprint will permanently be reduced to zero.

Bob knows that your vote, like your life, is insignificant, but Bob would like your vote anyway. As Bob likes to say,

"Your vote is unimportant, so why not give it to Bob?" He knows that your vote, while otherwise worthless, can provide temporary value, but only if placed in the right hands—Bob's hands.

Bob knows that our only hope for affecting our existence is if we can accelerate our own demise. With votes like yours, Bob promises to support unwinnable wars with guaranteed cataclysmic losses. Bob understands that only by succumbing to a quick and fatal end can we save our youth from the melancholy of a prolonged existence. No more fretting about complex problems that can't be solved. No more wasting energy on fruitless battles for power over nothing. And no more living in delusion.

Vote for the only meaningful change possible in a meaningless world. Vote for mass self-destruction. Vote for Bob.

CELEBRITY

WHEN YOU PRETEND, YOU CAN BE A STAR.

My Biopics, Reviewed

The life story of a man, whether a hero or scoundrel, is told by his actions. To capture his story in one telling, the challenge is to choose moments from a lifetime of events that are faithful to the truth and the spirit of the man.

———From the prologue of my unfinished screenplay Gandhi II

1 FOR 2

**** INSPIRATIONAL

An improbable story about the winless season of a fourth-grade basketball team competing in the Chicago Archdiocese Resurrection Youth League. McQuinn's 1-for-2 free-throw performance leads the Tigers to their closest defeat of the season and is the highlight of this remarkable film about trying your best.

THE WIZARD OF ST. NICHOLAS

*** SOULFUL

Witness the hectic two-day run of the St. Nicholas eighth-grade class production of *The Wiz* through the eyes of an apathetic chorus member. The unique all-white casting of a musical tailored to African-American culture provides the backdrop to this semi-rhythmic romp by a group of reluctant preteens who are just glad to be missing Social Studies.

BACKUP MAN

**** SURPRISINGLY MASTERFUL

Superior acting by Pitt captures the essence of being a data-entry clerk on an IBM System/36 in the mid-1980s. Pitt's re-creation of McQuinn's ability to balance receivables while performing tape backups is awe-inspiring.

DREAM WEAVER

** DISAPPOINTING

Would like to have seen more of McQuinn and less of his female co-stars. Sure, the montage of women he has bedded with his mind is impressive, but the story would be more compelling if we saw these women's fantasies about *him*.

FANTASY LEAGUE

*** A REAL WINNER

Captures the drama of a fantasy football season as seen through the eyes of a first-year player. From the excitement of draft day to the cruelty of premature elimination, experience the ups and downs of an office draft league as if you were managing your own make-believe team.

DRIVE HOME

*** PURE ADRENALINE RUSH!

McQuinn's struggle to best his own record for fastest drive time home from his work is a pure thrill ride. Like *Speed*-meets-*9 to 5*!

BEST BUY

**** DAZZLING

Spacey as McQuinn is at his best. Obsessed with finding the perfect family-room flat screen, we follow McQuinn's journey from the World Wide Web, where he learns the jargon of HDTV, to the floors of an electronics retailer, where he uncovers the truth in the LCD/plasma debate. When he finally decides on a model with the perfect combination of features and value, you share his triumph. And when prices mercilessly drop just weeks after his purchase, you wallow in his pain.

Dan McQuinn

Doing It The Right Way

**** Must See

Chronicles McQuinn's meteoric 15-year rise from an engineering intern to a junior associate engineer and his refusal to succumb to the petty politics of his peers.

No Longer Serving Breakfast

*** Courageous

Inspiring story of one man's struggle against the tyranny of a fast-food behemoth and its inflexible breakfast-menu schedule.

Close Call

*** Triumph of Spirit

McQuinn's poignant reaction to the events of September 11 is the most moving account yet of this darkest day in American history. Watch McQuinn on his morning commute as he unwittingly listens to a Flock of Seagulls CD in repeat mode as the Twin Towers fall. And when he later recounts how he had only three years earlier flown from the same Pennsylvania airport as the ill-fated United Airlines Flight 93, you will get chills.

THE GRADUATION GIFT

*** SENTIMENTAL SURPRISE

When Dan gives a moderately expensive set of earrings to the daughter of his supervisor as a high school graduation gift, co-workers and people he just met are taken aback by Dan's benevolence and good taste. A classy film about a classy guy.

Dan McQuinn

Couldn't Have Done It Without You

Thank you. Thank you. Please sit. No. Thank you. This is too much. Really. Thank you. No. Please sit. Thank you. This is embarrassing. Really! Please sit. Thank you. Thank you.

So many people are responsible for my being here today … no, please sit. … Unfortunately there's not enough time to thank them all. So in advance, my apologies to anyone I miss. I do ask that you indulge me for a few minutes to express my humble gratitude to a few of the special people who helped me get here today.

At this point, I would have asked my parents to stand up but I can't, because they are *not* here tonight. They could have attended, if they had confirmed their invitation sooner. Apparently, Fort Wayne, Indiana, has more pressing matters than the Academy Awards. Fortunately, I had no problem filling their seats, as I have numerous friends who appreciate the significance of being nominated for the Motion Picture Association's highest honor. They also know the meaning of the letters RSVP. And they would never try to hide behind words such as *incapacitated* and *diabetic coma*.

Kids Say the Cutest Things When They're Drunk

Mom and Dad, even though you are not in attendance, I still would like to thank you for all that you have done for me. Thank you for smothering me with a stable home life. Thank you for suffocating me with expensive schooling. And thank you for forcing upon me an outdated value system. In case you did not notice, Harold and Emily, I am being sarcastic—displaying a keen wit that I did not learn from either of you. To this day, I am amazed that I have been able to blossom into the success I am in spite of being held back by your primitive concepts of child rearing.

I'd also like to thank Wayne High School coach Leo Carter, my sophomore year physical education instructor, who inspired me to greatness by showing me firsthand what it means to be a human failure. Coach motivated to me to work hard to avoid becoming like him, a pathetic loser whose only joy comes from forcing a person of infinitely more talent to run laps in sweltering heat until the onset of vomiting. Because of coach Carter, I was able to steer clear of mediocrity and push myself to achieve greatness—and I still can't do a boy's push-up.

I'd also like to express my thanks to the entire female population of the Indiana State University, who, by resisting my advances, failed to entrap me in a cloying relationship so detrimental to an emerging artist. Your loss is my gain.

I would also be remiss if I did not remember the legends who helped shape my cinematic vision, the big three of film-making: Stanley Kubrick, Martin Scorsese and Irwin Allen. To these visionaries, I am forever grateful. While my work has often been compared to these greats—"Biggest disaster on film since Irwin Allen," said Roger Ebert of the *Chicago Sun Times*—one needs to remember that these moviemakers have had the benefit of first mover's advantage. I'm sure if I'd been born earlier I could have grabbed the low-hanging fruit of the great movie ideas and made a *Taxi Driver*, a *Clockwork Orange* or even a *Towering Inferno*, albeit with the inclusion of my signature trademark: the talking parrot.

Of course, without you, my fans, I would just be another genius toiling in obscurity. But with your devotion and constant appetite for everything me, I am a genius toiling in a 40,000-square-foot estate—and that's just my summer home. Critics have called my fan base lemmings, but I prefer to think of you as lemmings with taste. After all, without your blind devotion, my film could not have obtained the visibility necessary to capture the Academy's best-picture award, a first for a three-minute YouTube video.

Finally, I'd like to thank the person most responsible for my being here today, myself. Without my talent, drive and vision, I could never have become the overwhelming success I am today. No one was more dedicated. No one more selfless and no one more deserving—than me. What makes my accomplishments even more amazing is that through it all, I've been able to retain my natural humility and grace. Bravo, Howard J. Bittleman, bravo! I couldn't have done it without you!

Dan McQuinn

Now Playing

Cameron Williams (Jason) is tickled to be back in Dubuque playing our hero. Hailing from Sioux City (also the home of my ex-girlfriend Jenny), Cameron has appeared in numerous local TV and radio commercials, including a brilliant performance as the Muffler Answer Man. Has also enjoyed the honor of singing the national anthem at the Des Moines Civic Center for Wrestlemania 2006.

Kate Winslow (Liza) is returning home to the Midwest after a stint with the long-running Canadian production *Insomnia! The Musical.* Previously a member of the Quad City players, a musical improv troupe focused on the issues of medical negligence. With flowing auburn hair (very similar to Jenny's), her dream is to one day sing for the surgeon general.

Mel Claussen (Grandpa Joe) is on loan from the Shady Pine Adult Care Center, where he is playing the role of Pee-Wee for an in-house production of *Boys Town.* Born without eyelids, Mel views his impairment as a showbiz asset, having garnered a steady stream of extra work playing zombies and surprised spectators.

Kids Say the Cutest Things When They're Drunk

Monica Freeman (First Waitress) loves live theater, especially after working for two years at Chuck E. Cheese's with only robot actors. Monica likes to practice her lines with a coconut carved to look like a human head. Eerie, since Jenny's favorite shampoo is Suave Tropical Coconut.

Terrence Flatley (Dr. Benjamin) is a big fan of scientific curiosities, sporting the largest collection of bovine tumors in the state, which reminds me of an inside joke that Jenny and I used to share. I won't try to explain. You'd have to know Jenny like I do to understand. A true method actor, Terry practiced for the role of Dr. Benjamin by drawing six pints of his own blood in a two-week period—leading to a three-week hospital stay.

Jacob Carter (Jason's Butcher) owes everything, including his acting career, to the Lord. "Jesus died so I could do theater," proclaims Jacob. Currently writing a Christian crime drama for the Nashville Network. Favorite places on Earth are Bethlehem and any Baskin-Robbins. Makes all his own costumes and hates sorcery of any kind. Says he saw Jenny with an older man at church once who he thinks was her father. Jenny's father lives in Nova Scotia, so he must have been mistaken.

Kevin Quinn (Monsignor Kerrigan) loves a good fight even when under one of his rare bouts of sobriety. Kevin landed the role of Monsignor Kerrigan when he demonstrated his ability to recite the Lord's Prayer in Pig Latin. (Jenny speaks French!) A true minimalist, Kevin shuns electronics and does not even own a phone, making him just as difficult to reach as you know who. When not holding court at the bus depot, Kevin can usually be found in the stairwell of the Eighth Avenue Parking Garage sleeping in a puddle of his own urine.

Vanessa Jameson (Vanessa) is happy to be in a production where she can wear clothes. Can still be seen dancing every Thursday night at Diamond Ray's in Davenport. When not performing, likes long beach walks, champagne bubble baths, horseback riding, etc. Believes in total commitment (are you listening, Jenny?), as evidenced by her willingness to do *anything* for a role. Hopes to settle down someday and marry a doctor, which explains her frequent clinic visits.

Wayne Levy (Cousin Christopher) is no stranger to live audiences, having starred in his own one-man play *The Testicle Monologues*. An avid biker, Wayne likes his roles as raw as the chaps he wears when riding his Suzuki. Voted the "best up-and-comer" by *The Bettendorf Village Voice*, Wayne enjoys working with young actors and supports creating "openings" for fresh talent. Wayne is also very trustworthy and, unlike some people, would never forget to return a borrowed Stevie Nicks CD even after a breakup.

Vance Razer (The Kid) believes in living fast and leaving a good-looking corpse, which is the explanation he provided police last week when they discovered a human torso in the trunk of his Saturn. Until further notice, Kyle Henley will thus be playing the part of The Kid. Kyle's performance tonight will mark his first appearance on our stage, including rehearsals, as Vance's regular understudy is still considered missing.

Nathan Hamilton (Mario) has entertainment in his blood. His father once was an understudy for Jim Nabors, and his mother wrote a children's play explaining existentialism. Recently a guest entertainer for Six Flags St. Louis, Nathan likes to find the angst in his characters, whether he's playing the Son of Sam or Yosemite Sam. When not performing, Nathan can be found driving very fast in his red Jeep, just like the one that is now always parked each night in front of Jenny's townhouse?

Molly Kidderman (Aunt Sarah) is thrilled to be playing her dream role. "I always wanted to be a foulmouthed old hag–and now I am." Her rant in Act I culminating in the line "Thanks for ruining my life, you ungrateful cunt" really strikes a chord with this theater-watcher. Isn't it always the beautiful ones that make you want to drink heavily and start fires?

Sam Hutchinson (Attorney Rooney) plays a bottom-feeding lawyer like those who profit from the propagation of gutless restraining orders. For Christ's sakes, I was only trying to get my CD back. Besides, the patio door was wide open! You'd think after devoting nearly four months of your life to a person, you'd be allowed to check up on them once in a while. Since when did it become a crime to care? I am, though, truly sorry about leaving the gate open to her neighbor's yard. I would have been more careful if I knew their dog was unleashed, and I will pay for any burial expenses. Sam also has a dog (living) named Buster.

From the Notebook of Matt Damon

June 9, 1994

Another session where I write and Affleck smacks his chewing gum while pondering whether he's using enough moisturizer. I swear, if his dad weren't paying the rent ...

June 12, 1994

Affleck thinks WE should rewrite script with Will as a geography prodigy. Ben claims he's much better at geography than math even though he still gets lost on the subway. Finally backs off when I show him that neither Harvard nor MIT offers a major in map-reading.

June 16, 1994

Affleck promises to write scene between Will and his psychiatrist. Shows up with a verbatim excerpt from a "Facts of Life" script with the names Blair and Tootie scratched out and replaced by Will and Sean. Nevertheless, Ben's best work so far.

June 23, 1994

Never has a man been so obsessed with his own nipples as Ben Affleck. Whenever struck with a story idea, shouts "Me nips—they are a-tinglin'!"

June 28, 1994

Today's nipple tingle: Instead of Sean missing Carlton Fisk's home run in Game 6 of the 1975 World Series to spend time with the woman who would eventually become his wife, Ben thinks it would be more dramatic if Sean missed Game 7 and Carlton Fisk hits the series-clinching home run. Never mind that this would require rewriting history so that Boston and not Cincinnati would become World Series champions, prematurely reversing the legendary curse of the Bambino. Sure I'd love to see the Sox win it all, but if I'm going to pay $8 to see "Platoon," I don't want to see the U.S. win.

July 7, 1994

Affleck just saw "The Lion King" and now wants to adapt "Good Will" to animation. Spends rest of day humming "Hakuna Matata" and drawing stick figures trying to capture essence of characters.

July 13, 1994

Now he wants me to add a dance routine. Is it a sin to will a head injury on another person?

July 17, 1994

Find Ben at keyboard, where he is "sprucing up" screenplay by adding colored fonts and inserting clip-art pictures of kittens. When I find a wad of his gum clogging the floppy drive, I lose it and smack him in the skull. He flails at me like a girl, and I totally kick his ass. I finally relent when he pretends to choke on his gum.

July 18, 1994

Strange, but my fight with Ben is the cathartic breakthrough I needed and I now know what I need to do. Unbeknownst to Ben, I now maintain two screenplays: the real version, purged of exploding robots and talking unicorns, and *his* version.

August 15, 1994

Ship a copy of real screenplay to Castle Rock. Ben continues to work on his version, which has taken on a life of its own. Not wanting to be tainted by association, I suggest we adopt a pseudonym because that's what cool writers do. Rename working draft "Patch Adams."

Sept. 2, 1994

Receive a call from agent. Castle Rock loves "Good Will"! They would like to set up a meeting but first want us to make a few minor changes. They think script needs more action and would like the Will character to be more high tech, or, as they put it, "something with robots and explosions … "

Kids Say the Cutest Things When They're Drunk

WHY I AM THE FUNNIEST PERSON ALIVE

I'VE STUDIED COMEDY MY WHOLE LIFE. When other kids were playing with their Lite-Brites and Slinkys, I was glued to the family Zenith studying the comic masters. Whether the slapstick of Bob Denver or the timing of consummate straight man Lyle Wagoner, I've learned from them all. And from this wellspring of comic knowledge I've drawn one undeniable conclusion: I am the funniest person alive. Period.

You're probably saying, "How can a guy who's never hosted an HBO comedy special be placed above comic legends such as Chris Rock or Robin Williams?" It's simple. While the Steve Martins of the world have an army of gag writers who write their every line, I am funny all the time without the help of any Hollywood joke men. For example, just yesterday I bent over to pick up a dropped Oreo and pulled a thigh muscle. Not so funny, huh? Well, while most people would have whimpered like a wounded rape victim, I seized the opportunity to display my comic range and mustered in my best Danny Glover, "I'm getting too old for this shit."

And if you accompanied me for a day, you would observe many such bits. If my wife asks me to make her toast, I'll respond, "Where's the recipe?" If I find an empty stapler at work, I'll tell our secretary, "It's time to call Staples." And when standing at a urinal, I'm always the first with "Boy, this water sure is cold."

Not limited to quips, I like to fuse my humor with props and pratfalls. Like a master chef who constantly experiments with new recipes, I am always scanning the environment for new ingredients for my comedy. Like the time I spotted the boy next door's skateboard in my driveway. I could have easily just picked it up and handed it to his father, but I seized the opportunity to mine comic gold. Pretending to trip over the forgotten toy, the hilarity only heightened when, writhing in "pain," I screamed threats of a lawsuit. When I finally came clean later, the look on the faces of my neighbor, his lawyers and the judge were priceless. Jim Carrey, eat your heart out!

Ever since I can remember, I've been making jokes. At 7, I hid in a J.C. Penney's fitting room and giggled for three hours while my mother had the mall security search for me. And in high school, I perfected my celebrity impressions. In fact, my imitations were so flawless that I had my freshman Spanish teacher convinced that Charles Manson was calling her from prison. *Dios mio*!

To be the funniest requires more than just spontaneous wit. That's why, priding myself on my comic preparation, I always carry with me a plastic sandwich bag filled with feces. Anyone who witnesses my "Waiter, I think there's a pile of shit on my plate" routine invariably risks a laughter-induced hernia.

The bag of excrement is not my only prop. Just ask my son how his Cub Scout troop was rendered speechless at their last pancake breakfast when I presented their den mother with a "gift basket from the kids" featuring a footlong dildo.

Being the funniest person alive, though, is not without drawbacks. I have so much talent that I often make people laugh even when I am not trying to be funny (You should see how much my wife laughs during intercourse!). I am also constantly confronted with other comics' jealousy. Why else, after meeting me only once at a book signing,[1] would Jeff Foxworthy have a restraining order placed on me?

But the biggest problem is that being funny undermines my being able to pursue my true passion: quantum wave theory. No matter how revolutionary my findings or how developed my research, the scientific community just will not recognize genius when it's wearing a fake nose and glasses. That's why from here on out, it's no more jokes for me. I am going to focus on my research, and when I receive my Nobel Prize, we'll see who's laughing. Pretty radical, huh? — Got you!

---

1. His not mine.

Dan McQuinn

MISS YOU

Danny McQuinn
4638 W. 84th Place
Chicago, IL 60629

Nov. 30, 1981

Dear Danny,

   I am writing to thank you for such a smashing weekend. I can't remember the last time the band and I had so much fun—and with a Yank, no less!

   Keith was just saying how touring can be such a drag and we really have to meet new people. What a stroke of luck, then, running into you at that sandwich shop by our hotel (I believe you called it the Wendy's?). I could listen to your stories about the characters you meet all day and was totally taken aback by the complementary Frosty. How lucky to have a job where you get to eat free sweets all day! (At least when you're manager ain't look'n!)

   After years of performing in front of millions, I can't believe I finally got to meet our No. 1 fan. Not only did we meet, but we were able to hang out together all weekend! The best part was how you were not stuck up and such a good listener. I can be such a bore with all of my petty problems. You're so right that I need to be more assertive and plan more *ME* time. What a breath of fresh air to talk to someone who really gets it, unlike most our fans who just want something from us. By the way, enclosed are the autographed pajamas you requested.

Please also be sure to pass along our thanks to your parents for their hospitality. My old man never would have chauffeured us around town like your dad did, let alone help us haul our equipment to a gig. His station wagon is so roomy! Charlie is especially thankful, as he was dreading the thought of dragging his drum kit to the stadium on public transport. We also really appreciate you both taking the time to show us the sites. Usually, we only see a city from the back of a crowded tourist bus, but what a thrill to get a private tour from a couple of real natives. Where else would we have learned that Chicago has the world's largest water-filtration plant? I can't wait to get back to London to see the look on Jerry's face when I tell her that one.

Hopefully next time we visit you'll be old enough to join us at the blues pubs without having to worry again about your American bouncers. They can be such wankers! It didn't spoil our fun, though, eh? We had a much better time hanging out in your basement playing the Atari Space

Invaders. And Bill and your little sister seemed to hit it off so well. Besides, if we had stayed out, we would have just ended up disco-hopping with some dull fashion models who only want to get high and shag—and totally missed your mum's brownie treats!

We would have also missed our jam session. Man, I never would have thought of using a Wurlitzer on *When the Whip Comes Down*. What a sound! I also still crack up every time I think of you "cutting one" during Keith's solo, only to respond, "Well, excuuuuuuse me!" How do you come up with such lines? If you don't mind, I think I might borrow that one for the chat shows.

I wish all our tour stops could be as fun as last weekend. Right now we're stuck doing a show in your Hawaiian Islands. Good luck finding a proper chip shop in this dreadful place! Everything has pineapple in it. Yuch! While we're here in the Pacific, I'm looking into buying a few islands to build a new recording studio, so the chap who does my accounts says we probably should add a few more tour dates or repackage another "greatest hits" collection. If we do swing by your city again, I'll definitely give you a jingle.

In the meantime, please send my best to your family and thank your mum again for the treats. Ronnie would also like to pass along his apologies for her bathroom hand towels. For the record, he insists those were brownie stains! Trapper John is now coming on the telly, so I got to run.

　Cheerio!

　Your best mate, Mick

Dan McQuinn

WILL SMITH HATERS NEWSLETTER

Welcome to the second edition of the Will Smith Haters Newsletter—the only publication dedicated to despising the career of rapper-turned-actor Will Smith. I know in our inaugural launch nine months ago I promised a quarterly printing schedule, but I just have been so busy! As the sole writer, editor and publisher, I am completely responsible for all content, production and promotion while still fulfilling my full-time duties as a Sam Goody senior sales associate. Nevertheless, quality will not be sacrificed for the sake of timeliness, as I am committed to producing the best newsletter possible even if it means missing an occasional issue or two. As the reader, I am sure you will understand, as you benefit the most from the superior content.

Of course, the best way to assure that you don't miss a single issue of disgust toward America's most overrated film star is with an annual subscription. Why worry about erratic delivery schedules when you can sleep well knowing that a fresh newsletter will arrive in your mailbox whenever I get around to printing the next edition?

With the holidays upon us, subscriptions also make perfect gifts for any friends or co-workers to whom you may have been lending copies. While our advertisers—make that advertiser (thank you, Vic's Dry Cleaning!)—appreciate the widened distribution, it's only fair that all readers pay their fair share for enjoying "the best newsletter ever for exposing the fraud of Will Smith."

LATEST NEWS

As of this writing, the Stale Prince's latest film, *I am Legend* (someone is full of himself!), has grossed over $500 million worldwide, proving once again that the general public loves watching disasters. In this movie, Will and his dog are the last non-zombie inhabitants of New York City. While the thought of a New York without New Yorkers does have allure, two hours of watching Will sass-talk with a German shepherd will turn any moviegoer into the walking dead. What really makes this movie totally intolerable, though, is that Will plays a research scientist (can a Nobel Prize be next?). I'm not saying that *People* magazine's 14th-most beautiful person in 1998 isn't smart enough to be a scientist. In fact, on his own Web site, Will claims that he had high enough SAT scores to get into MIT but he was "just not interested." Yeah and if I were more focused on my studies, I could have invented the space shuttle. I just think the movie would have been more palatable if Will had been cast in a more believable role—oh, I don't know, say a brainless gym teacher or a vain actor who's so insecure that he's compelled to put his SAT scores on the World Wide Web.

PURSUIT OF HAPPINESS UPDATE

Am I the only one who noticed that Will's 2007 Oscar nomination was for playing the father to his own son! Not exactly stretching your acting muscle, huh, Will? Besides landing him a best-actor nomination, the casting of his 9-year-old son helped cement his reputation as one of Hollywood's best family men (puke) while garnering him an even greater haul of the film's gross. Talk about your pursuits of happiness. (That's right. Like the rest of the English-speaking world, I spell *happiness* with an "i.") Worst of all, the expansion of the Smith dynasty to his hammy child ensures that we will be subjected another generation of Smith overacting.

OBAMAMANIA

Speculation has run rampant that Will Smith will play Barack Obama whenever a movie is made about Barack's life. Will, however, may have his own political aspirations and has been quoted as saying he could be president himself in 15 years if he puts his mind to it.

Many also consider him the front-runner to play Harris if *Barney Miller–The Movie* ever makes it to the big screen. At the time of this printing, it was still unclear how long it would take him to prepare for this role *if he put his mind to it.*

MAILBAG

—Jim Barnes from Louisville, Kentucky, writes in with a great idea for boycotting the movie *Ray*. Technically, Will Smith was not in *Ray*, but if you decide to start a Jamie Foxx haters newsletter, count me in!

—Virginia Simmons from Lufkin, Texas, has a son Richard who is a huge fan of the newsletter and is currently serving his second tour of duty with the U.S. Army Rangers in Iraq. Mrs. Simmons says her son has started his own Bagger Vance Haters edition, which is a huge hit with his squadron. Way to go, Richard, and remember to send those royalty checks!

—And to all the Ku Klux Klansmen who keep writing, thanks for your letters. While this is technically a hate-group newsletter, anyone who has seen my Bernie Mac DVD collection can vouch that I am not a racist! My disdain for Will Smith is based purely on objective review of his body of work and a burning desire to wipe that smug grin off his goofy face. I don't want to see him lynched, but a string of box-office busts a la *Wild Wild West* would sure be fun.

WILL SMITH CHALLENGE

Match the quotes below with the Will Smith character who says them:

"Aw, hell no"	Agent Jay, *Men in Black*
"Aw, hell no"	Captain Steve Hiller, *Independence Day*
"Aw, hell no"	Oscar (voice), *Shark's Tale*
"Aw, hell no"	Muhammad Ali, *Ali*
"Aw, hell no"	Hancock, *Hancock*

God

Everyone needs a higher power to blame.

CAIN'S NEW GIRLFRIEND

Since Adam and Eve were the first human beings, biblical scholars have long debated how civilization could develop without their children intermarrying.

Cain: Mom, Dad, this is Jessica, the girl I've been telling you about.

Eve: Er, uh ...

Cain: Isn't she pretty?

Eve: She's very pretty, but ...

Adam: Son, what your mom is trying to say is that we already know Jessica.

Cain: You guys know each other? That's great. What a small world!

Adam: Real small.

Eve: What your dad means is that Jessica is your sister.

Cain: What?

Eve: While you were out roaming the desert for the past few years, we had Jessica and raised her.

Cain: This happens every time I meet someone!

Eve: If you called occasionally ...

Cain: You guys are always telling me to be fruitful and multiply?

Adam: Son, of course we want you to meet the right girl and ultimately give us grandchildren. We just would expect you to find someone outside the immediate family.

Cain: That's easy for you to say. You've got, like, 50 kids!

Eve: There's no reason to be insolent.

Cain: Are you pregnant again?

Adam: Your brother Abel would never talk to his mother that way.

Eve: Speaking of Abel, have you talked to him lately? It's not like him not to call.

Cain: No, I haven't seen Abel ...

Send in the Frogs

ADVISER: Pharaoh, the land is overrun with frogs!

PHAROAH: Frogs?

ADVISER: Yes, just as Moses predicted.

PHAROAH: The cute little green animals with the long tongues?

ADVISER: It's a terrible plague ...

PHAROAH: They don't even have teeth.

ADVISER: But your highness, they're so icky!

PHAROAH: Can't we just step on them?

ADVISER: I suppose ... but we're only wearing sandals!

PHAROAH: You go tell Moses that if his God is going to intimidate the house of the Pharaoh, he's going to have to muster up something more than a few tree frogs!

ADVISER: Very well, sir.

Dan McQuinn

One day later

ADVISER: We heard from Moses, your majesty, and he says his Lord got your message concerning the frogs and if we don't let his people go, he will be sending an even more powerful plague to inflict us.

PHAROAH: So what does he have in mind? Wolves? Tigers? Bigger Frogs?

ADVISER: No, sir. ... Gnats!

Inscriptions from Jesus' High School Yearbook

I'm the first person to sign your yearbook! Just like you predicted when we were running laps—"May the last be first and the first be last …"

    Levi from PE

Hope you enjoyed our favorite Latin teacher—Roman Fingers. (Ha Ha)

    Love always,

    Bathsheba

Remember in biology when you brought that pig we dissected back to life? I will never forget the look on Mr. Samuel's face!

    Stay real,

    Benjamin from the house of Joshua

Study Hall was a lot of fun. Sorry I called you a gay boy so much.

>Mitch the Canaanite

You're so nice, it's no wonder you're so popular. I hope someday people will want me as much as they want you ...

>Barabbas

Loved all of your wacky parables. You are too funny!!!
>Your friend from homeroom,
>Hannah

Jesus, you have a great future as a carpenter. I hear the Romans are hiring cross makers.

>Demetrius from Shop

We'll probably never see each other again. At least we won't have to sit next to stink-breath Issachar anymore. Have a good life.

>Zechariah

Hope you can *cum* to graduation. It will be great to *jerk off* our caps and *unload* them into the air.

Always pulling for you,

Yankmeedic Tilithertz

Thanks for letting me cheat off you in Religious Ed. You really know your Scriptures! Good Luck!

Rachel, daughter of Hezron

Don't ever change, but if you do, do it in front of me! Sorry, I thought this was a girl's yearbook.

Big Judah

Your mom is such a MILF. Just kidding. (not really)

The Mad Whacker

Glad the year is over and we don't have to put up with Mr. Hannibal's bullshit anymore. See you at the chariot races!

Ben Hur

Dan McQuinn

It was great having you on the swim team. We could not have taken state without you. You really "walked all over" our competition!

Matthew

Sorry about prom. I did not mean to "forsake you." I really did have leprosy that night.

Mary M.

> Roses are red.
>
> Violets are blue.
>
> You're such a good friend.
>
> Even though you're a Jew.
>
> Have a good summer shithead!
>
> ——Petronius

Friends for life.

Judas

GOSPEL WRITER'S GROUP FEEDBACK

STRONG DIALOGUE WITH MANY memorable lines. Loved the "It would be easier for a camel to enter the eye of a needle ... " bit. Reminiscent of early Carnac: "May the fleas of a thousand camels infest your armpits!"

Solid story with good arc. I just had trouble believing your protagonist. While I love that you give Jesus magical powers, I just thought he was *too perfect*. He cures lepers, heals the deaf and even raises the dead! We get it. He's very helpful. Try making him more realistic by giving him a flaw or two. How about a speech impediment? Delusions of grandeur? Or maybe he's a recovering sex addict?

Also, whatever happened to the Joseph character? We find out that he is not Jesus' real father in the first act and then we never hear from him again. This could have been such a good reveal. Why give it away so early? Think *Empire Strikes Back*. Would the payoff have been the same if Luke had learned the identity of his father before he met Princess Leia? This twist was built up for two whole movies! Instead of dismissing Mary's husband, use him to escalate the conflict. What about a scene with Joseph and the Holy Spirit?

Imagine the tension between the cuckolded carpenter and Mary's mysterious suitor.

Character development of the disciples could also be stronger. We know little about them, and those that we do get to know are one-dimensional: Doubting Thomas, Matthew the Tax Collector, Judas the Traitor, etc. Why not take the traits from each of the disciples and combine them in a smaller number of more complex characters? Instead of 12 apostles, why not give Jesus three well-developed good friends?

Thought the "Manasseh begets Amos and Amos begets Josiah ... " routine was overdone and unnecessary. Kind of feels like you're padding your word count.

This is a technical comment, but I noticed that you had quite a few footnotes. Almost every line had a superscript! I could not find the actual notes, though, so please include in your next draft. Consider streamlining, as too many notes can be distracting. While footnotes can provide valuable background information, whenever possible try to incorporate back story into your main text, as it makes for a tighter narrative. Better yet, if not critical just eliminate.

Also, I would highly recommend putting your last name on all your drafts. While your modesty is admirable, you're better off nowadays being safe than sorry. You'll need to give your full name anyway when you go to copyright. Besides, I've seen at least three other pieces with almost identical story lines. I'm not sure who has the original story rights, but you should act quickly and definitely consult an attorney.

The parables are wonderful little nuggets! What an imagination! While I like the idea of stories within stories, why have Jesus tell us these tales when you can show us? Figure out a way to incorporate these anecdotes into Jesus' life and let the reader experience the action right along with him.

False endings are always tricky, but you handled it very well and absolutely *nailed* the death scene. For a second, I thought you were going to use a dream sequence to bring the hero back, but I was glad to see you not rely on this tired ploy. I also loved the bread crumbs you dropped with Jesus warning about the temple being destroyed and rebuilt in three days. When I realized that Jesus himself is the temple, I almost fell off my chair! And his mysterious disappearance into the heavens at the end provides a satisfying finale while leaving the door wide open for a sequel.

Overall, I thought this was a good first draft. I don't think it needs a major rewrite, but with a few tweaks you should have a story you can market. Probably not mass appeal, but it should draw interest from the supernatural-fantasy crowd. I would definitely check on that attorney thing, though.

Keep writing. The world needs your talent!

Dan McQuinn

What God Said to Me the Last Time I Prayed

— Danny? Is that you? It's been such a long time.

— I'm not used to you contacting me directly. Usually your thoughts are full of heaving breasts and chocolate.

— Oh, there you go again. Sorry I mentioned it.

THE GOOD, THE BAD AND THE MIDDLING

A self-assessment using Jesus Christ and Jim Croce's *Bad, Bad Leroy Brown* as benchmarks.

JESUS CHRIST	BAD, BAD LEROY BROWN	ME
Born in a stable in Bethlehem.	From the south side of Chicago, the baddest part of town.	I'm from Chicago, too!
Women visited him while nailed to a cross made of tree limbs.	All the ladies call him Treetop Lover.	Females have described portions of my anatomy as twiglike.
Known by men as the Son of God.	All the men just call him "Sir."	My favorite song is *Sir Duke*.
Also known as the King of Kings.	Badder than old King Kong.	Bad at Donkey Kong.
Rode on a donkey and walked on water.	Got a custom Continental and an Eldorado, too.	Drive a Saturn and a Toyota mini-van.

Jesus Christ	Bad, Bad Leroy Brown	Me
Befriended prostitutes while wearing robes.	Now Leroy, he's a gambler and likes his fancy clothes.	I can't hold my liquor and have trouble finding clothes that match.
Received gifts of gold, frankincense and myrrh.	Likes to wave his diamond rings in front of everybody's nose.	Like to show off my sport watch.
His Father and the Holy Spirit are always with him.	Got a 32 gun in his pocket for fun and a razor in his shoe.	Have a cell-phone with a battery that does not hold a charge.
Jesus was a teacher who taught through parables.	Learned a lesson about messing with the wife of a jealous man.	I'll never learn.

DEATH

ALL YOUR FAULTS ARE FORGOTTEN, BUT SO ARE YOU.

THE FIRST TELEPHONE CONVERSATION WITH MY MOTHER AFTER NUCLEAR ARMAGEDDON

— Hello? Danny? This is your mother.

— Oh, hi, Mom.

— I was just calling to see how you were doing after the Armageddon.

— I'm fine. I was going to call you, but I wasn't sure the phones would be working ... you know with 95 percent of the planet destroyed and all.

— Our phone is working.

— It sure is ... clear as a bell. Sounds like you're just next door. You're not just next door, are you?

— No. We're at home.

— Good. You and Dad are OK then?

— Your dad's sinuses are bothering him.

— They always bother him. He should get them fixed.

— Maybe. What we really need to get fixed is our garage-door opener. It doesn't seem to be working. Is yours working?

— Yeah, my garage-door opener is working. Did you try changing the batteries?

— Batteries?

— The remote for the garage door should have batteries. Probably AA.

— Oh, we didn't try that. We thought that maybe the radiation did something.

— That's possible, but I'd try the batteries first. On second thought, things are still pretty dicey outside. Maybe you should just keep the garage door shut.

— That's probably a good idea. Oh, your dad wants to know if your car is running OK?

— My car? Yeah, it's fine. Does he need a ride somewhere?

— Oh, no. He just wants to remind you to get the oil changed.

— I got it changed right before the blast, so I should be OK. You know, Dad doesn't need to remind me to change the oil. Jiffy Lube puts a little reminder sticker on your window.

Kids Say the Cutest Things When They're Drunk

— They think of everything nowadays.

— I don't think it matters. With the highways still engulfed in flames, I don't think I'll be driving anywhere soon.

— It's so hot out! We just keep the shades closed and the air on all day.

— Probably a good idea. It should also help with the flesh-eating zombies.

— The who?

Dan McQuinn

WHEN DEATH GETS PERSONAL

Starting today, due to previously announced consolidations of our editorial team, the death notices will be written by the Tribune Classified and Personals writing staff.

Audrey Wilson, 86, died in her sleep Wednesday dreaming of her ideal mate, an affectionate and spontaneous romantic who is preferably Catholic. Survived by her twin sister, Evelyn, SWF, also Catholic.

Benjamin Powell, 56, was called to eternal peace yesterday while cleaning his collection of German sidearms. A self-proclaimed "lover of Lugers," once bought a pistol fired by Hermann Goering. Survived by spouse who will pay cash for all WWII souvenirs, including Nazi daggers. Call Vivian at 312-299-4185.

Vincent T. Hudson, 66, retired colonel USMC, veteran of the War in Vietnam, the Persian Gulf War, and an unpublicized conflict in Singapore during the Reagan administration, died of congestive heart failure. Described by friends as "down to earth" even before knowing of his burial on Saturday.

Maureen Holman, 70, seeks open, honest relationship with her maker. Does not have to be Prince Charming, but please, no Shreks! A lover of fine dining, sports and long walks on the beach, Maureen hopes to do all of these and more in the afterlife.

Edward Ostrowski, 38, died Thursday after a two-year battle with colon cancer. Loved boating, camping and driving his red Corvette; 2004, CD, sunroof, low mileage, $16K or best. 312-935-6688.

Bob "Corky" Watson, 60, liked to keep it real and believed the eyes were the window to the soul. Once went to a hypnotist to stop smoking and now is only smoldering (LOL). Survived by three adult children and four ex-spouses.

Ken Kramer, 49, loving husband of Sandra, believed in open relationships with like-minded singles and couples. Fond of adventure and group activities, Ken and Sandra loved entertaining in their home with friends both new and old. Interment at Blessed Trinity Cemetery, Mount Prospect. Walk-ins welcome. Consenting adults only.

How I Imagine Necrophilia Starts

— Wow! That was the best sex ever. Was it good for you?

— Don't want to talk bout it?

— That's OK. Let's just cuddle.

— Oh my God! You're stone cold.

— Too bad. That was really good sex ...

DEAR LOVED ONES

Dear Loved Ones,

As you may already know, my life is over. If you are reading this letter, it can only mean that my attorney, Saul, has upon my death delivered this letter to you per my instructions. I guess I finally learned my lesson about (Saul, insert form of death here), but at least I do not have to worry about repeating that mistake again. Ha Ha.

I am a little saddened to be leaving a little earlier than expected but feel no sense of tragedy. I lived a fruitful life, and my only regret is that I could not take you, my loved ones, with me.

Barb, I know that Saul is not your favorite person. But if you can look past his extramarital affairs and indictments, you will find that Saul can provide a treasure trove of advice, advice that you will desperately need in the coming months. After all, his people have a long history of coping with suffering and, more important, know a thing or two about managing a nickel. Besides, any counsel he can offer has to be better than listening to your sister.

Barb, you have been my confidante, friend and lover. I've cherished my time with you, and our last three years together have quite possibly been the best of my life. (The six years before you started taking Prozac is another story.) When I look back at my life, I realize that none of my accomplishments could have been possible without your raising our children and doing my laundry. And while the loss will surely be difficult, you can take satisfaction in knowing that my mother was finally wrong—we did not end up in divorce court.

Now that you have the task of raising two young children on your own, you will be expected to act as both a mother and a father. This challenge should be especially tough given that I have always been the kids' favorite. The first time one of them shouts "I wish it was you that died!" just remember that it's really just their way of saying they miss their dad.

To my son, Jack, I will be missing more of your soccer practices than usual. Hopefully, my spotty attendance to date has prepared you well for this moment. You will also now be the man of the family and as such take on certain responsibilities. In the coming months, your mother will no doubt have more adult male guests than usual. Remember that in spite of this parade of testosterone, I will always be your father, and your job is to remind your mother and her houseguests of this fact. Mark my territory whenever possible. If anyone tries to sit in my chair, throw a violent tantrum. And if anyone parks in the driveway, don't forget the key-on-the-door trick I showed you. It should be a real hoot.

And to my daughter, Rose, while I know my passing will be hard on you, please don't forget that this unforeseen tragedy affects your dance instructor as well. Cindy—excuse me, Miss Jacobs—will also be experiencing loss, as she will likely miss my presence at your practices and recitals. If she appears to be withdrawn and edgy, just remember that she, too, needs time to heal and this period of grief is not "all about you." To help her mourn, please let her know that she is welcome to stay at our summer cottage whenever she likes. She should already have a set of keys.

And to my parents and my dog, Corky, I never imagined that any of you would outlive me. I have, thus, not prepared anything to say other than "See you soon."

Finally, I would like to address the question that all of you are most interested in: "What happens to my money?" As you know, medical technology is advancing nonstop, and the possibility exists that someday science may find a remedy to whatever it was that forced my early demise. Thus I've decided to take advantage of the miracle of cryogenics and have my body frozen until a means to revive me is available. As there is no guarantee of when this breakthrough will occur, my revival chances are increased the longer I can stay in a state of suspended animation. As such, my final wishes are that the assets from my entire estate be liquidated and invested for the express purposes of funding the ongoing expense associated with freezing and reviving my body.

Within the next few days, Saul will be contacting you with regard to the immediate sale of our home and possessions. Undoubtedly, you will feel entitled to an ownership claim to some items. Heads up—this is the time to start digging out those receipts. Don't fret, though. Saul has determined that touching your Social Security benefits is legally impossible, ensuring that the public safety net can provide adequately for each of you until we can be reunited.

Nevertheless, I encourage all of you to move on with your lives. When I do return, I expect things will be different. For example, I will have aged chronologically but not biologically. As such, I expect to be seeking companionship from someone more compatible with my body's age, as I will have been "stiff" for a long time. Rose, maybe one of your playmates will fit the bill?

I have to stop writing now. Saul just arrived, and he is going to explain to me how I can collect unemployment benefits while I'm frozen. Remember, even though I'll be packed in ice, I can still have guests. Feel free to visit, but please no flash photography.

With Loving Memory,

Dan

P.S. Do not erase my iPod.

Epilogue

ENDINGS ARE ALWAYS HARD TO ACCEPT, so final, so definite and often filled with regrets. I know that if I could write this book again, I would say more nice things about the people I love, and I'd use a word processor. But endings can also bring new beginnings, which lead to new middles, more new endings and more regrets (although the regrets are usually not new). Quite a beautiful and vicious circle, really.

You may be wondering how the end of this book can be a new beginning. Simple. By telling every soul you know about this funny little read you've discovered, you can create new beginnings for others.[1] By doing so, you will come across as smart because you've read a book, and that's what smart people do. And if you want to appear very smart, write online reviews, blog, tweet, poke and do all the other stuff smart people do on the Web after they've looked at

---

1. And if you didn't find this book funny, what's wrong with you? I mean, who reads a humor book all the way to the end if they don't find it funny? If this sounds like you, seek professional help, as you really have a serious problem. To avoid further embarrassment, lie and tell everyone you found this book very funny.

their porn. So rather than considering this the end, think of this as the beginning: the beginning of your opportunity to promote *Kids Say the Cutest Things When They're Drunk* to the four corners of the Milky Way galaxy, or at least to all your Facebook friends.

THE BEGINNING

Proposed Titles for this Book that were Rejected

Another Nobel Prize Winner

Why Bother? We're All Going to Die Anyway

A Children's Guide to Autoerotic Asphyxiation

Naked Pictures of Mohammed

Complete Nonsense

Whatever You Do, Don't Tell Your Parents

The Lactation Consultant's Handbook

The Complete Wisdom of Western Civilization

My Penis Is Sore and the Cat Is Bleeding[1]

A Military History of Wisconsin

When God Farts

By Now, I Thought We'd Have Sex Clones

The Biggest Piece of Shit Ever!

---

1. This may have been a statement of fact and not a title submission, but when brainstorming, there are no bad ideas.

—SPECIAL BONUS—
BOOK CLUB DISCUSSION QUESTIONS

1. To what extent did you feel sympathy for the book's characters? Which character would you most likely have an adult consensual relationship?

2. How did the author's font selection reveal his world view? Would you feel different about the work if written in Helvetica 16?

3. Does the book's title speak to you? Do you often have conversations with inanimate descriptive headings?

4. Do you think the author is a moral person? Would your answer change if the book was priced at $20.95?

5. Do the bonus book club discussion questions help illustrate any of the book's themes? Provide other examples in literature of how "filler" material can trigger nonsensical thought.

6. Rate *Kids Say the Cutest Things When They're Drunk* from 9 to 10.

Acknowledgements

I would like to thank my new friends at The Editorial Department, especially Peter Gelfan, Ross Browne, Doug Wagner, Christopher Fisher, and Jane Ryder, for their advice and encouragement. I feel so lucky to have found them. If you're crazy enough to try to write a book, I'd definitely look these folks up.

I'd like to thank all my friends and instructors at Second City whose encouragement and advice gave me the confidence to keep writing, especially Rob Chambers, Spike Kunetz and the late and dearly missed Mary Scruggs. I'd also like to thank Chris Lackner, whose feedback greatly improved this book.

Many thanks also to Dennis Marcellino for his wonderful cover design.

Jumping into the way-back machine, I'd also like express my gratitude to Mr. John Kroc and Mr. John Lynch, the best high school literature teachers ever. They opened my eyes to what is possible through writing while being damn funny as well.

I'd also like to thank my next-door neighbor whose sevens look like nines and whose mail-order packages I regularly receive in error. I'm really enjoying the foot massager. Do you have any plans to order the optional moist-heat warming foot wraps?

And most of all, I'd like to thank my wife Barb, and not-so-drunk but still cute kids, Rose and Jack, who give me more joy than the laws of physics should allow. They have always encouraged my writing, even when it contributed to my neglect of them.

Finally, I'd like to also thank my parents, who have always put my interests above theirs and still have nothing to show for it.

And for all those people I've forgotten to mention or, worse yet, insulted in this book without their permission, please forgive me.

About Dan

DAN MCQUINN LIVES IN THE western suburbs of Chicago with his trophy wife, Barb, and gold-medal children, Rose and Jack. They also have an awardless German shepherd whom they consider part of the family, regardless of what the IRS says. When not writing defamatory essays about his family, Dan enjoys watching baseball games and Spanish soap operas.

Dan attended the Illinois Institute of Technology, where he studied electrical engineering yet still installs camera batteries upside down. He also received an MBA in finance from DePaul University, which helps him buy new cameras. He now works in the telecommunications industry yet has never been able to explain to another living being what he actually does.

After the birth of his children, Dan had a poor man's midlife crisis and took up writing. Starting with Denny's comment cards, he worked his way up to indignant letters of complaint and eventually enrolled in Second City's comedy-writing program, where he specialized in knock-knock jokes.

Dan McQuinn

Dan's favorite books are *One Fish, Two Fish, Red Fish, Blue Fish* and any catalog where you can buy X-Ray glasses. Dan never expects to retire, planning to devote his sunset years to tasteful seminude modeling.

Contact Online:

www.danmcquinn.com

Email Dan at dan@danmcquinn.com

www.ingramcontent.com/pod-product-compliance
Lightning Source LLC
Chambersburg PA
CBHW061640040426
42446CB00010B/1504